＝MY＝
Big Bottom
Blessing

≋MY≋
Big Bottom
Blessing

How Hating My Body Led to Loving My Life

Teasi cannon

WORTHY
PUBLISHING

Published by Worthy Publishing, a division of Worthy Media, Inc., 134 Franklin Road, Suite 200, Brentwood, Tennessee 37027.

HELPING PEOPLE EXPERIENCE THE HEART OF GOD

eBook available at www.worthypublishing.com

All Scripture quotations are taken from the New King James Version. Copyright © 1982 by Thomas Nelson, Inc. Used by permission. All rights reserved.

Published in association with Wayne Hastings Company, LLC

ISBN: 978-1-62090-373-5

Cover Design: Christopher Tobias, Tobias Design
Cover Photo: ©Darren Greenwood/Design Pics/Corbis
Photo Illustration: PixelWorks Studios
Interior Design and Typesetting: Susan Browne Design

Printed in the United States of America

To Carli, my sweet beauty from ashes

And they overcame him by the blood of the Lamb and by the word of their testimony, and they did not love their lives to the death.

Revelation 12:11

CONTENTS

CONTENTS

ACKNOWLEDGMENTS

Thank you, thank you, thank you . . .

To my precious man, Bill. You are my best friend. You are my dream-come-true. Thank you for moving heaven and earth to fight for my heart and for loving to spoon.

To my amazing babies: Carli, Ben, and Sam. I know it's a nerdy mom thing to say, but my heart bursts with love, joy, and everything divine when I think of you. Thank you for the gift of yourselves, for every hug and every sweet kiss on my cheek. They fill my tank.

To the people who directly enabled me to write and publish this book, huge thanks:

Dawn and JT Taylor. For your love and friendship, for introducing me to the life-saving truths that are layered into these pages, and for faithfully standing by the operating table while God performed some major reconstructive surgery in my heart.

Jack Frost (who is reading this from heaven), Trisha Frost, and the entire Shiloh Place ministry team. For your disarming transparency, heart-gripping understanding of the Father's love, and willingness to share it. God used your ministry to save my life.

Allison Allen. For our near-daily talks about everything under the Son, your never-ending encouragement to give God time, and the eternal blessing of a loving and kindred friend.

Phil Stoner. For being the very first to say, "Write that book," and being generous enough to read through my very raw first attempts. Your support lit the fuse.

Toni Birdsong. For your laugh, your zeal, your lovingly brutal honesty, your amazing gift of encouragement, and the hours of your precious time spent helping me make this story better one chapter at a time.

Wayne Hastings. For seeing something compelling in the pages of my manuscript, feeling led to send it to a few friends in book publishing, and then patiently guiding me down the roads of my brave new world. I couldn't ask for a more patient and kind agent and friend.

To Byron Williamson and his over-the-top incredible team at Worthy Publishing:

- Kris Bearss. Oh. My. Gosh. Thank you for reading my manuscript and liking it. Thank you for your support of not only this book, but of me. You are an amazing executive editor, and I thank God for you always.

- Sherrie Slopianka. Thank you for your support and more-than-generous help with all things social networking. I think I've finally passed Facebook 101.

- Thank you, Rob Birkhead, for your marketing genius; Morgan Canclini, for your kindness and help; Jeana Ledbetter, for graciously leading me through my very first book contract; and for all the amazing creatives who designed the cover and interior of this book.

Thank you, Susan Tjaden, for rounding out the edges and bringing an expert shine to the pages of my story. I'm so thankful for you. You are a sweet and incredibly gifted editor.

Thank you, Marika Flatt and Tolly Moseley at PR by the Book, for your support, wisdom, and for helping me get the word out about *My Big Bottom Blessing*. You are both amazing.

To the generous and gifted people who took their time to read and endorse this book: Wynonna Judd, Allison Allen, Steve and Sarah Berger, Michele Pillar, Lisa Patton, Nancy Reece, Trisha Frost, Pete Wilson, Jenni Catron, Constance Rhodes, Lisa Harper, Toni Birdsong, and Cindi Wood. I know you are all very busy, so thank you from the bottom of my heart.

Thank you to my pastor, Steve Berger, and his precious wife, my friend, Sarah. For nearly half my life you've shown me what it looks like to serve and honor God no matter the cost. Thank you for loving me and supporting me over all the years.

Thank you to these bosom friends I've been blessed with over the years: Christina Broadwin, Suzy Foley, Michelle Rajcic, Tracy Dekaney, Colleen Daly, Barb Mahy, and Jodie Grenead. I adore you all.

Thank you for the friendship, encouragement, counsel, and wisdom of the following people: Rick and Diana Cua,

Jeanie Davis, Dave and Cheryl Buehring, Sarah Richmond, Kelley Arnold, Wes and Linda Yoder, Lark Foster, Robin Morrison, Camille Piland, Tami Olin, Pam Hastings, Meg Cox, Amy Lowry, Melinda Myers, Anne-Marie Helmsworth, Diane Spencer, Carol O'Rourke, Suzanne Brown, Rachel Bradley, Brittany Jenkins, Byron Spradlin, Kara Christenson, and Kathy Rowland.

Thank you to all the pastors, elders, and committed Grace Chapel family who have loved me in so many ways.

Thank you to my Gootee and Cannon family. I love you all. Thank you to my incredible mom and dad, who always believed I would write a book someday and loved me enough to speak words of life and hope over me year after year. I'm so glad God chose you to be mine. And Jenny Fann, my sweet baby sister, I'm so proud of you. Thank you for loving me all these years no matter what.

To my grandma, Johnnie B. Parker. Thank you for handing down my big bottom genes. I adore you, and I can't wait to dance with you in heaven some day.

And to You, the most worthy One, my Father God. I thank You for my whole life and with my whole life. You are my everything, and I give You everything.

INTRODUCTION

Does this book make my rear end look big?

You probably won't be able to answer that question until after you've turned the last page, but hopefully your answer is yes. If it is, more glory goes to that crazy good God of ours—the One who truly turns the most unlovely of things into treasure.

Here's the main gist of how it happened for me: even after giving my life to Jesus and becoming a "good Christian girl," there was a lot of work left to be done in my life. It took me awhile to figure out that this is true for everyone. There isn't a person who stands up from the altar after saying one simple sinner's prayer and walks away perfected. Not you. Not me. Not anyone. It's just a beginning—the starting point of our Christian expedition.

It seems like an obvious truth. Logic would tell me that change takes time. But somehow, almost subconsciously, I thought that simply being a Christian meant that everything should be just fine. After all, the Bible tells us that we can do all things through Christ and that we are more than conquerors—old things are gone and so on. The problem was I wasn't seeing all the evidence in my life, especially in the area of my weight. No matter what I tried, I could never seem to get thin, and that nearly ruined everything. Nearly.

My weight on the scale led to such an agonizing weight of emotional pain in my heart, which led to a total breakdown, which (ironically) led to the very adjustments that saved my life. As these adjustments were made, things started getting better. I know that statement sounds annoyingly simple. So, let me be clear: some of the adjustments were quick and easy, but some took lots of time and were quite painful.

Now, the reason I can't keep this story to myself isn't because I feel the need to share my pain. No one would want to read a story filled with only pain. No, I want to share the story because I love my life now, whereas I used to be miserable. Because I love my friends now, whereas I used to be jealous and bitter. And — perhaps most miraculously of all — I love my body now, whereas I used to hate with a capital *H* — *Hate* — myself beyond words.

I have a feeling the same can be said of you. And as you read this story, I hope you will discover that you are not alone in your pain, no matter how great or small. I hope that you can get healing for even the deepest wounds in your heart, and that you can learn to silence the community of voices/lies in your head as truth takes over.

As I tell you how it all happened for me in the pages to come, I'll also share a little of my poetry, a taste of my journal entries, a lot of my findings, and some heartfelt prayers. Oh, and along the way I'd like to introduce you to some of the characters who claim my head as their residence.

Welcome to my experience of the goodness of God.

My
Big Bottom
Blessing

ONE

A BUM DEAL

There are enemies all around us
Seeking to destroy
They come to tear our hearts apart
And take away our joy.
Some are just plain bothersome,
Some invoke great fear.
But none are near as devastating
As the enemy in the mirror.

•••

Imagine yourself standing in front of a mirror right now—completely naked. Can you say that you love who you see? Believe it or not, I can.

Now you're probably thinking one of two things: either this lady has a perfect body, or she's a total liar. Wrong. In fact, at the writing of this book I am about fifty pounds heavier than society deems appropriate, and I promise the declaration is no lie. Hopefully you will find this easier to believe once you've read my story. It is an unraveling—or maybe a roller coaster—but it's a tale that ends ever so triumphantly.

As you can probably surmise by now, I have not always been okay with my body. In fact, most of my life *disgust* would have been the appropriate word to define what I felt when looking in the mirror. Research shows I'm not alone. A recent *Glamour* magazine poll revealed that 97 percent of women have cruel thoughts about themselves each day—thirteen times a day on average.[1] And sadder still, 90 percent of high school junior and senior girls diet regularly, even though only 10 to 15 percent would be considered truly overweight.[2]

VALUE INFLATION

This obsession we have with weight and physical appearance is crazy—especially from a Christian perspective. Think about this: the value that has been placed upon being thin is not a value that has been given by God. In fact, the Bible is pretty clear that what matters most to the Lord is the appearance of the heart. Although being healthy is important, God is far more concerned with the amount of love we are showing than with the firmness of the thigh we are showing. So, who do you think is behind this value inflation? Could it be the Father of Lies, the devil? Who else would want to keep us distracted and weighed down by things that matter so little? Who else wants us to hate the very flesh God made?

It's one of the world's biggest tragedies, really. Millions of women like you and me take their first steps of each day into a bathroom where a lie/mirror is waiting to tear them down. For some the object of ridicule is a nose that is too large. For others it is a web of wrinkles. For me it was always my weight.

Looking back on my earliest years, I don't remember there being even one season in which I was happy with my body. Painful awareness of my larger size came as early as elementary school. Kids were cruel. Being teased in grade school feels . . . well, you remember how it feels, don't you?

And we all remember the little saying about how sticks and stones might break our bones, but words . . . now those can *never* hurt us. Denial in its earliest stages, don't you agree? I used to stick my little chest out—along with my tongue—while reciting this cheeky mantra in the face of many a bully, hoping it would magically erase my humiliation and fear. But it didn't have the power I'd hoped for. The words just plain hurt. In fact, they stuck to my heart like glue.

Isn't it sad that the hurtful words of our past are the ones that have the most sticking power? I have several flash-bulb memories of my parents hugging me and telling me how smart and beautiful I was. I have vague memories of teachers telling me what a pleasure I was to have in class. But the memories of what the bullies said . . . now, those are crystal clear.

All I need to do is close my eyes for a moment, strap on the seat belt of my mind, and I'm instantly transported back to the fourth grade. I'm doing my best to hold down the position of class caboose as our line makes its way to PE, my all-time least favorite class. Then the sixth graders round the corner heading our way. I can feel my little heartbeat quicken and my palms begin to sweat. I know what is coming. I know *who* is coming: Johnny. Blonde-haired, freckle-faced, chase-me-off-the-bus Johnny and his hideous sidekicks.

Now in order for you to fully understand the humiliation that would soon flood my soul, I need to offer a quick pronunciation key. My maiden name is Teasi Gootee, prounounced TeaSee Goaty (like goat). It was not at all easy having a name like this in elementary school, especially because it was almost always pronounced Teeeezee Goooody.

So out of Johnny's mouth come (at hall-filling volume, of course) the knife-like words with the adhesive power of super glue: "Teeeezee Goooody has a greasy bootie." Over and over again he'd say it. Every time he saw me, he said it. And others joined in the fun. I can still feel the phantom pains in my stomach.

Trying to stand up for myself only made me feel even more ridiculous. All I could do was shout, "No I don't. I just took a bath!" That didn't help anything.

I remember every detail of times like those. Good news is, I survived . . . and personal hygiene is priority to this day.

MEET MY TRAINER

It was during those early school years that I came to know a powerful character who would play a huge role in my life for several years to come. Her name is Trainer. Now, one thing you must know about Trainer is that she is invisible. Even I can't see her, but I can certainly hear her—and I'm the only one who can. In fact, she lives in my head, but that doesn't hinder her one bit. What she lacks in physical existence, she more than makes up for in verbosity. Some of our earliest conversations would go something like this:

> TRAINER: Teasi, sit up straight. The fat roll on your stomach is bulging out like crazy.
>
> YOUNG FAT GIRL: Oh, okay. (*Sits up as straight as humanly possible.*)
>
> TRAINER: Now, look at how wide the expanse of your thigh is on that bench compared to Christina's. Disgusting! Put your feet up on your toes or something to keep those legs from pressing down on the seat.
>
> YOUNG FAT GIRL: Oh, okay. (*Sits in ridiculously uncomfortable position in order to decrease thigh width by an amazing half an inch.*)

I remember getting so fed up with Trainer every now and then that I would humiliate myself just to torture her. This would involve something akin to me being nude in front of a mirror while jumping up and down repeatedly just to watch my rolls bounce. I knew she hated my fat, and in my mind this would really show her. But my antics didn't do anything to help my self-image.

And of course my best friends in school were always skinny chicks. I may not know you personally, but I bet if you hated your nose as a young girl, your best friend had a perfect one. It's got to be one of those laws of nature: "Whatever a young girl lacks and wants more than anything, her best friend surely has."

All through my school years, my closest friends were beautiful (a God-given attribute I can now—finally—applaud in others). This made Trainer even angrier the older I got. Man, she would get really upset with me:

TRAINER: Oh! My! Gosh! Teasi! No boys are going to like you like they do Michelle if you can't get some fat off that rear end. (*Trainer was never one to hold back.*)

TEEN FAT GIRL: I'm trying. I'm doing aerobics every day and running miles.

TRAINER: Yeah, but you can't get enough of those honey buns, now can you? Just have to keep stuffing that fat face! If you could just stop eating, maybe you could get a boyfriend.

TEEN FAT GIRL: Well, today all I've had is a half cup of Cheerios with one-fourth cup of skim milk, three M&Ms, a spoonful of peanut butter, three small sips of a grape slushy, a cherry Life Saver, half of a ham sandwich with light mayo on thin bread, and an apple.

TRAINER: Don't forget the three crackers.

TEEN FAT GIRL: Oh, yeah. And three crackers. (*Hangs head in shame*).

Oh, it was torture. No matter what I did to lose weight, I was always several sizes larger than other girls. It didn't make any difference to me that my body fat percentage was right where it should be. What mattered was the number on the scale.

And soon the only other thing that mattered was having a boyfriend.

YES OR NO

I got my very first boyfriend in seventh grade, and I was elated. I still remember the thud of the tightly folded note as it dropped on my desk. Once I opened it, I could see that my name was fourth in line after three others which had been scribbled out, but that didn't matter to me. I ignored those names and focused on the words, "Will you go with me, check *yes* or *no*." Shaky and giddy with excitement, I checked in the affirmative and tossed the note behind me, trusting it would land in the right place. I felt like I was in a dream. I was now the girlfriend of Kurt, one of the popular kids.

Our first date was a trip to McDonald's. His dad picked me up in his brown El Camino, and we were off. As soon as his dad pulled out of the parking lot, leaving us for an hour of quality time, Kurt took my hand and asked me if I wanted to take a walk first. *How romantic,* I thought. *Wow, this is better than I could have imagined.*

We walked along the railroad tracks that ran behind McDonald's, talking and laughing about school stuff. Once we rounded the first bend and were sufficiently out of view, Kurt leaned over to kiss me. My first kiss. I was floating. That is, until I felt his hand traveling up my shirt.

"No, Kurt. Don't do that," I said. And the kissing continued. Until I felt his hand trying to undo my pants.

"No, Kurt. Stop. You'll respect me for this when you're older."

As you can probably predict, Kurt didn't stop to look at me with deep appreciation for my mature composure, as I was certain he would. He only laughed in my face, told me we were through, and headed back to McDonald's. It was a silent ride home. I didn't even get a cheeseburger.

MEET MY REFLECTION

I did a pretty good job protecting my private parts until tenth grade, but by then my self-esteem had plummeted while my pant size continued to rise. My best friend wore a size zero then, and I wore a size 10, which meant I had no chance at all of attracting a boy with my looks. Welcome to my promiscuous years.

As if Trainer wasn't bad enough, after several years of doing what seemed necessary to get attention from the opposite sex, another prominent character entered my life. Meet

Reflection. Like Trainer, she was disgusted with me, but for different reasons. Trainer hated what I looked like, but Reflection hated who I was. And she was very good at bringing up the things I was trying hard to ignore in order to simply live with myself:

REFLECTION: How could you end up with that guy? You really have become quite the slut.

YOUNG FAT WOMAN: No I'm not. Please don't say that.

REFLECTION: I thought you were going to wait until you were married. What happened to that little dream, huh?

YOUNG FAT WOMAN: It died, I guess. (*Wipes away a tear.*)

We all have times in our lives that we regret, but I really feel sad when I look back on those years of my life. The desire to be a virgin on my wedding day was always present in my little girl heart. The problem was, that desire did not come with an understanding of *why* I wanted it. So, when the pressure came to give up that dream, there was no arsenal with which to fight. It took me years to understand purity was a God-given desire—one He puts in all little girls' hearts, and some girls are strong enough to protect it. But for some of us, the desire gets buried by the lies of this world, and we are tricked into giving ourselves away too soon. Oh, God *tries* to protect our hearts with His instructions, doesn't He? He knows that sexual intimacy is a gift—a priceless gift meant to be enjoyed by a man and a woman who will never leave each other. It is a deep sharing of oneself, not meant to be experienced with those who do not understand.

In my ignorance and in my pain, I had given myself away one piece at a time until Reflection couldn't even look at me anymore.

REFLECTION, MEET JESUS

Reflection and I hated each other for many years. Then Jesus came. I was twenty-one when He entered my life for keeps, and I will never forget that time.

For me it happened basically like this: I sank to a new, wretched low. None of my friends wanted anything to do with me—including my heartthrob. Completely alone and crying for days, I finally realized something needed to seriously change. In other words, it finally dawned on me that I was doing a *reeheeheally* (thank you, Jim Carrey) bad job of directing my life. Miraculously, the Jesus I met casually as a little girl came knocking on the door of my heart again and lovingly asked, "Can I have my throne now?" I couldn't hop down fast enough.

Once comfortably seated in His rightful spot, Jesus asked me to start going to church. I had never actually attended a real church in my life. Don't get me wrong, my family did believe in God, and we were part of an organized religious group for years. But we left once the leaders started interpreting the Bible in some less-than-orthodox ways. Years later I spotted the group's name on a list of cults to avoid. All I could do was shrug and thank God that at least there hadn't been poisoned Kool-Aid involved.

Along with giving my Sundays to God, some other serious changes started happening in my life—changes that startled many who knew me. I immediately stopped working in a bar. I immediately stopped partying and sleeping around. I immediately started listening to Amy Grant music (definitely not cool in southern Cal at the time). I was absolutely charged and excited about what Jesus was offering me: forgiveness and unconditional love.

It took a little while for Reflection to understand that by giving my life to Jesus, my past failures were as good as gone. In God's eyes, it was as if they had never happened, and that was good enough for me. Truth was what the Bible had to say about me, that "Though your sins are like scarlet, they shall be as white as snow. . . ." (Isa. 1:18). I was holding my head up high for the first time in my life.

Even so, there were several tense conversations:

REFLECTION: There is no way Jesus loves you. Think about all the filth you've been a part of!
YOUNG FAT WOMAN: I know. I know, but He really does love me. I can tell . . . in my heart.

REFLECTION: You can tell in your heart? Now, isn't that sweet. Priceless! Are you really that stupid?

YOUNG FAT WOMAN: I'm choosing to believe what God says to me in the Bible. That's final. I get a do-over.

After seeing my resolve, Reflection lightened up on me a bit. But not for long.

REFLECTION AND TRAINER CONSPIRE

Right around my twenty-second birthday, Tennessee called my name. My parents and siblings had moved there a while before me, and I could feel them tugging on my heart. So I loaded up my Toyota Celica (the kind with the cool flip-up headlights) to the brim, and left California behind. It was a grand trip—just Jesus and me. It was an epic adventure.

But not long after settling in, my adventure took an unexpected turn. At first the turn looked good: I met a cute guy . . . in church! He had big muscles, a winning smile, and (most importantly, of course) he was an usher. Surprisingly, he started to take an interest in me, and we began spending time together.

We talked a lot, and day by day I began to see that under those big muscles he was broken. He had issues—big issues—mainly with drugs and alcohol. Some pretty clear signs led me to wonder if I should leave the relationship behind. My parents saw the signs, too, and pleaded with me to get out while there was still a chance. But Trainer and Reflection had another take on the situation:

REFLECTION: Who is she to expect perfection from anyone? I mean, just think about all those horrible things she did when she was younger. Come on!

TRAINER: I agree. Plus, look at that rear end. She's lucky this guy even finds her attractive.

REFLECTION: And, Jesus would want her to sacrifice for this guy. After all, isn't that what Christianity is about? Being willing to give up everything—even if it means being miserable?

TRAINER: She's only gonna get fatter over the years. She better take this chance while she's got it. There might never be another guy who would find that body attractive.

REFLECTION: You're right. She should stick with him no matter what!

So, it was settled. The guy needed to be loved, and the perfect one for the job was me. I chose to stick by my man. And even though he was in drug and alcohol treatment only months before, I walked down the aisle with him and became his wife.

I knew I'd made a mistake the moment I said "I do."

Of course a baby was on the way shortly after the honeymoon. Even though the news sucked the wind out of me initially, my sweet baby Carli saved my life. She's my positive note, my bright spot, my beauty from ashes, and all the other metaphors that represent amazingly sweet things that can come from devastation.

But my husband only got worse and worse. Oh, he tried to stay sober between bouts of jail and treatment, but he was still broken. His brokenness came out in abuse toward me, and after I could let little Carli see no more, she and I left. It didn't take long for him to start sleeping around, which made it clear to me our relationship was unalterably shattered, and with that another childhood dream died. My story was not going to end with a happily ever after.

Reflection made sure the scarlet letter "D" was securely fastened to my identity. I was a young, fat, divorced single mom. (Had I been one to use the classified ads to find a date, they could just call me YFDSM. Great. No thanks.)

> REFLECTION: Great! Look what you've done. How do you expect God to ever use you for anything now? You're a . . . divorced . . . woman. (*Looks away with disgust.*)
>
> YOUNG FAT DIVORCED SINGLE MOM: I don't know. (*Tears.*)
>
> REFLECTION: You've really let God down. And no one will ever want you now that you're . . . you're tainted!

TRAINER: And look at you! You're even fatter now than ever. And look at all those stretch marks. Now, that's pretty! (*Three short, sarcastic grunts.*)

YOUNG FAT DIVORCED SINGLE MOM: I know. I know. Just leave me alone. Please! Leave me alone.

Failure. My relationship could officially be added to the other one-third of Christian marriages that ended in divorce that year. What an accomplishment!

There was no getting around it. With all the heart and soul I could muster up, I threw myself into being the best mom possible, going back to school to become a teacher in hopes of becoming an adequate provider for my baby girl. There was a lot of alone time spent with Jesus, since He was the only one who would have me. And after many, many months of Jesus pursuing me, I found out He was the only one I really needed. He loved me desperately, even though I was . . . fat.

WHAT ABOUT YOU?
NEGATIVE THOUGHTS EXPOSED

1. Stand in front of the mirror completely naked (not with your small group, of course). Write exactly what you think about yourself. _____

   _____

   _____

2. How do you think your answer from question one lines up with what God would say about you?_____

   _____

   _____

3. A recent *Glamour* magazine poll revealed that 97 percent of women have negative thoughts about themselves every day. How often do you have negative thoughts about yourself? _____

   _____

4. If you answered "every day" to question three, about how many times a day do you think something negative of yourself? _____

5. Do you remember the time in your life when your negative thoughts about yourself began? If so, when was it?

_____

_____

_____

6. Trainer (the one who hates your appearance) might not live in your head, but I'll bet you've heard a voice like hers. What is something typical you remember hearing from her? How did you reply?

   a. **TRAINER:** _____

_____

_____

   b. **YOU:** _____

_____

_____

_____

7. Reflection (the one who is disappointed with you as a person) might not live in your head, but you've probably heard a voice like hers, as well. What is something typical you remember hearing from her? How did you reply?

   a. **REFLECTION:** _____

_____

_____

_____

b. YOU: _____

_____

_____

_____

PEP TALK: NO DENIAL

Even though it is far less than pleasant to admit the negative self-talk that takes place in our heads, getting real about it is the first step toward silencing the voices we're sick of. Ignoring Trainer and Reflection (and any others who get their kicks out of deriding us) is not going to solve anything. We want those self-defeating voices to feel as exposed as a person in a porta-potty who forgot to lock the door. We want them to start worrying because we are ready for serious change. Today is the beginning of the end of business as usual.

FORWARD FOCUS: THOUGHTS

- Proverbs 16:3—Commit your works to the LORD, and your **thoughts** will be established.
- Isaiah 55:8—For My thoughts are not your **thoughts**, nor are your ways My ways, says the LORD.
- Isaiah 55:9—For as the heavens are higher than the earth,

so are My ways higher than your ways, and My **thoughts** than your thoughts.

- Jeremiah 4:14—O Jerusalem, wash your heart from wickedness, that you may be saved. How long shall your evil **thoughts** lodge within you?
- Jeremiah 29:11—For I know the **thoughts** that I think toward you, says the LORD, thoughts of peace and not of evil, to give you a future and a hope.
- Matthew 12:25—But Jesus knew their **thoughts**, and said to them: "Every kingdom divided against itself is brought to desolation, and every city or house divided against itself will not stand."
- Hebrews 4:12—For the word of God is living and powerful, and sharper than any two-edged sword, piercing even to the division of soul and spirit, and of joints and marrow, and is a discerner of the **thoughts** and intents of the heart.

TWO

A SECOND CHANCE?

I would have lost heart, unless I had believed
That I would see the goodness of the LORD
In the land of the living.
—KING DAVID (PSALM 27:13)

•••

Okay, so who's ready for a really sweet love story? I hope you raised your hand, because I think the next part of my tale will encourage you.

I took being a single mom very seriously. I worked several part-time jobs—things I could do with Carli—and went to school full-time. We had so much fun together, my little buddy and me. And I was doing my best to stay hopeful.

Now, chances are you, too, either are now, were at some point, or have a good friend who is a single mom. After all, according to the US Census Bureau, there are approximately 9.9 million single mothers in America, a number that has tripled over the last four decades.[3]

You also might know that the big issue for Christian single moms is trying to really be okay with it. Even more truthful: trying to be okay with the thought of not having help to raise your child, not having a man to love, not being held, feeling like you're a second-class citizen, always being alone.

The goal for the Christian single mom is to get to the point where God is truly enough. And I believe we all get there. Then we stop pretending. We admit that everything is not okay, and we cry out to that God—the one who way back in Genesis said Himself that it's not good for us to be alone. We expose what we believe to be weakness: a longing for companionship that just won't ever leave. And hoping He will understand that we love Him still, we dare to put words to our most private prayer: *Father, can I have another chance?*

UNFAIR GOD

Sometimes God's actions just don't seem fair. And I guess I'd have to say I'm glad. Let me tell you why.

There was once a little boy named Bill who grew up the youngest of eight children. He was a very good boy, and he told his mom and dad that when he grew up he wanted to be a "wuka [worker], a dahday [daddy], and a ministow [minister]."

As the boy grew into young adulthood, he made a very special decision. He would not mess around with dating a woman until it was the one he thought he would marry. He would not even kiss a woman until he found the one. And he stuck to it.

The young boy grew to be a man who looked back at his growing years with no regrets. He had not given his body to any, though there were many who would have had him, for he was quite handsome. He did not spend his time unwisely, instead he went to college, learned to build houses, fix cars, and play several musical instruments.

Then one day at church, Bill met a woman who intrigued him. Speaking to her casually here and there, he began to like her. In his heart he just knew she was the one. The one he had saved himself for all these years. The one he could give himself to completely.

Now, I bet you are already forming a picture in your mind of the woman Bill would choose. She would be a virgin, of course . . . blonde, blue eyes, perfect body . . . pure as the driven snow. Don't you think that's what he deserved after all that restraint? It would only be fair.

Well, guess what kind of woman God gave him? A young, fat, so-not-a-virgin, divorced single mom. That's right. He gave Bill *me*.

I CAN'T ACCEPT

I was just as shocked as you probably are to learn that such an amazing man wanted me. I thought God was playing a really cruel joke . . . on Bill! He was way too good for me. Reflection and Trainer both agreed:

> REFLECTION: It is just so sad for that sweet boy that he's ending up with you. Think of how many men have . . . well, you know. Gross!!!
>
> TRAINER: Just wait until he sees your body naked. He's going to be sick. And when he touches you . . . Oh, I just can't think about it. (*Holds hand over mouth as if stifling barf.*)

Even though I didn't want to say goodbye to Bill, I knew they were right. It wasn't a fair exchange. He was way above my caliber, and I just knew it had to be obvious to everyone. I wanted to have a serious talk with Bill about it all—to let him know he deserved better, and I would understand if he wanted to keep looking.

First, I needed to have a talk with God.

UNFAIR GOD (AGAIN)

> YOUNG FAT DIVORCED SINGLE MOM: God, how could You do this? How could You bring such an amazing man into my life—someone who loves You and loves Carli and . . . even loves me? You know I'm not good enough for him. It's just not fair for You to give him junk as a reward.
>
> GOD: You are right, it's not fair. It would be fair for you to pay the price for all the wrongs you have done. It would be fair for you to get what you

deserve. But . . . I chose to take care of it all for you. My love for you surpasses what is or isn't fair. My perfect, sinless Son bled and died for every one of your sins. Every single one. When I look at you, Teasi, I see you through that blood. I see Bill through that blood. You are both clean. You are a perfect gift for Bill.

For some divine reason, I didn't argue—not with God or myself. I just let those words sink deep into my heart, and somehow they muted all the objections waiting there. Who was I to tell God Almighty that Jesus wasn't enough? I didn't want to offend the Most High, so I decided not to have the talk with Bill. I would just have to trust God that I was a good match for him.

But I still didn't want Bill to ever have to touch my body.

THE DREADED CONVERSATION

Bill and I spent every possible moment together talking about almost everything—likes and dislikes, goals and dreams, hopes and fears. Well, I guess I'm really the only one who had fears, and they tormented me. Soon Bill could see that.

"What is bothering you?" he asked me one night.

I dreaded this conversation, and I was perfectly aware that it fit nicely in the "What Not to Talk About on a Date" category. But if I was going to possibly spend the rest of my life with this man, he would find out this information sooner or later. So, even though I was ashamed and felt like I wanted to throw up, I decided to show Bill the most vulnerable part of me. I had no idea what he would do with it.

"You have a beautiful, fit body, Bill, and you've waited all these years for God's best for you. How can I possibly be that?" I had to turn my eyes away for the next part. "I'm fat and scarred from having Carli, and I don't want you to see me."

When I looked back for his response, Bill's eyes were welling up with tears. He reached out and pulled me as close as he could—so close that I could feel his heart beating against my cheek. Gently pushing my hair away so that I would be sure to hear, he whispered into my ear. He told me that I was beautiful to him—more beautiful than he could put into words—that I was his precious gift from God. Nothing I had to say about it could change that.

To Bill the issue was settled. But Trainer . . . she was absolutely beside herself with anxiety, and she couldn't keep her mouth shut.

OPERATION WEDDING DRESS

TRAINER: You are getting married in three months! You don't have any time to lose.

YOUNG FAT ENGAGED-TO-BE-MARRIED SINGLE MOM: I know that! Calm down!

TRAINER: I will not calm down until you get at least

thirty pounds off of that big, fat body of yours. Can you imagine what you will look like in a wedding dress at your size? Do they even sell them that big?

YOUNG FAT ENGAGED-TO-BE-MARRIED SINGLE MOM: I know. I'm going to start running tomorrow.

TRAINER: You better. Make sure you run for at least thirty minutes to get into fat-burning mode. And stop eating carbs. No bread. No sugar. Do you understand me?

I understood, and I obeyed. For the next several months I worked my hardest to get weight off my body. And I actually succeeded!

When I finally went dress shopping, I was able to find a very pretty dress in what I considered a normal size, and after a near-death experience with maximum-restriction undergarments (I finally figured out how to get some oxygen to my lungs), I thought I looked like a decent bride. On the surface, that is. Under those layers, my stomach was waiting (and sagging) in the wings to make its debut. No amount of running around the track and away from Oreos had erased the evidence of pregnancy. And with the wedding right around the corner, there was nothing I could do about it.

THE BIG DAY

The wedding day finally arrived. I was so excited to become Bill's wife—so utterly amazed that God had blessed me with a second chance at love. And not only was it a second chance, it was completely different from my past. A fairy tale, really.

The ceremony was perfect. Both my dad and Bill sang to me—songs they had written. My sweet Carli was the flower girl—dressed almost exactly like me. We took lots of pictures. We gave lots of hugs. We ate cake. And Bill and I waited for the moment we knew was soon to come.

Even though my body was ever so ready to become one with Bill, it didn't want to be seen. Up until that very day I had been able to stay hidden, for we had done it right. We waited (much easier said than done). But that day I would have to reveal it all, and nervous doesn't even begin to describe the way I felt.

Being the perfectly sweet man that he is, Bill insisted on carrying me into the hotel room. As he bent over to scoop me into his arms, I said a quick prayer that he wouldn't break his back, and then I sucked in my stomach (as if that would make me lighter) and hoped for the best. He actually got me over the threshold. The prayer worked.

Waiting for us ever so invitingly on a small entry table was the "honeymooner's basket." In the center of the basket, a tall bottle of champagne stood calling my name. Oh, how I wanted to go to it and drink of its calming, confidence-boosting powers. But because my sweet virgin husband had never consumed more than a sip or two of alcohol, I didn't. I bravely plunged headlong (and sober) into my biggest fear: the bedroom.

THE BIG REVEAL

Bill went in before me, took his tuxedo coat off and tossed it gently onto a chair. Slowly I walked toward him, heading straight to . . . the curtains. After positioning them in such a way as to let in the least amount of light, I turned and went for the light switch. If I was going to do this, it would have to be in the dark.

Feeling my way through the room one piece of furniture at a time, I finally found my way back to Bill. It was time. Nothing left but the big reveal.

Bracing myself for the disappointment I was certain Bill wouldn't be able to hide, I shed my wedding clothes. He watched (as well as he could in the dark), and didn't do anything . . . but smile.

For a magical moment in time, I was able to forget my stomach and everything else I hated about myself, and I received the love Bill had waited so long to give.

HOW ABOUT YOU?
PRIVATE PRAYERS REVEALED

1. As Christians we're pretty good at praying the prayers that we should pray and keeping the things we're really hoping for hidden deep inside. You know what I mean, don't you? Those times when we pray, "All I want is *Your* will for me, God," while we secretly hope for a second chance at love, or that baby we've been longing for, or that opportunity we've been dreaming of. These are the things we are often afraid to put words to. What is your "silent" prayer? _____

   _____

   _____

   _____

   _____

2. Why do you think you've kept this prayer secret? _____

   _____

   _____

   _____

3. Do you think you could take a bold step in the direction

of faith and put words to your prayer in the space below? (This step is for us . . . God kinda already knows.) _____

_____

_____

_____

_____

4. Answer honestly: Do you think God is holding out on you? _____

_____

5. If you answered "yes" to number four, what kind of God do you think would hold out on you? _____

_____

_____

_____

6. God wants us to be honest with Him. He already knows what's going on in our hearts, but sometimes we don't. In the space below, write a note to God honestly telling Him what you're afraid He's withholding from you. _____

_____

_____

_____

_____

_____

_____

PEP TALK: NOTHING TO LOSE

Opening up about our most well-kept and secret prayers is a brave thing to do. It's brave because it requires a level of vulnerability that is far from comfortable. The good news is, however, that letting it all out to God is tremendously beneficial for us. When we open up our true self to God, we are walking in faith, and that faith builds upon itself. My mom used to always sing these words to my siblings and me as we went off to sleep: "Believing is the key to heaven, but faith unlocks the door."

But even more importantly, we've got nothing to lose by giving the real stuff to God. He's well aware of where we are, so to speak. It's just like in the garden when He asked Adam and Eve where they were. It wasn't that God was a loser at hide-and-seek. No, He knew exactly where they were. He just wanted them to know it. And He wants that for us. Honesty is a powerful GPS system. We've got to know where we are before we can determine how to get where we're going.

FORWARD FOCUS: SECRETS

- Deuteronomy 29:29—The **secret** things belong to the LORD our God, but those things which are revealed belong to us and to our children forever, that we may do all the words of this law.

- Psalm 44:21 — Would not God search this out? For He knows the **secrets** of the heart.
- Psalm 90:8 — You have set our iniquities before You, our **secret** sins in the light of Your countenance.
- Psalm 91:1 — He who dwells in the **secret** place of the Most High shall abide under the shadow of the Almighty.
- Ecclesiastes 12:14 — For God will bring every work into judgment, including every **secret** thing, whether good or evil.
- Jeremiah 23:24 — "Can anyone hide himself in **secret** places, so I shall not see him?" says the LORD; "Do I not fill heaven and earth?" says the LORD.
- Daniel 2:22 — He reveals deep and **secret** things; He knows what is in the darkness, and light dwells with Him.
- Matthew 6:6 — But you, when you pray, go into your room, and when you have shut your door, pray to your Father who is in the **secret** place; and your Father who sees in secret will reward you openly.
- Mark 4:22 — For there is nothing hidden which will not be revealed, nor has anything been kept **secret** but that it should come to light.
- John 7:4 — For no one does anything in **secret** while he himself seeks to be known openly. If You do these things, show Yourself to the world.

- 1 Corinthians 14:25 — And thus the **secrets** of his heart are revealed; and so, falling down on his face, he will worship God and report that God is truly among you.

THREE

THE DIE . . . IT

•••

As he vowed he would on our wedding day, Bill has loved me through my many ups and downs—ups and downs on the scale, that is. Not long after our honeymoon, those pounds I had so diligently worked to get off started creeping back on. And they stopped sneaking around once I got pregnant again. This is something I never heard: "Wow, Teasi, you don't even look pregnant until you turn to the side." No, no, no. When I was pregnant, even my eyebrows looked it.

I gained and lost more pounds than I can count in those first few years of our marriage, and Bill never once looked at me with anything but adoration and joy. I really believe he has a superpower—he sees right through my skin and extra cushion and straight into my heart. (I wish more men had that power, don't you?)

From the onlooker's perspective, it would have appeared I had it all. God had given me an amazing new husband who loved me unconditionally, we were both involved actively at our church (he was even asked to be an elder), our children were healthy and beautiful, and all our needs were more than provided for.

But if you could have seen inside my head . . . what a different story. The atmosphere there was much more chaotic. Despite all the love I had been given by Bill and by God, my thought-life could have been described best as a battlefield.

BATTLEFIELD: GROCERY STORE

Grocery shopping has never really been my thing. However, if a gal wants her children to eat, she must put on her big girl panties, grab a cart, and go for it. And because I personally find it the most challenging section in the place, I always started my shopping trips in the produce department. All the exotic fruits and vegetables — many I could not identify if my life depended on it — would greet me with quite a message:

FRUITS AND VEGGIES: Oh, *tsk, tsk.* You mustn't look at us. We are only to be purchased by the skinny and the healthy such as . . . her (*points to perfectly built woman in a short tennis skirt just grabbing a healthy cart full of produce after a morning match*). See her cart, so full of colorful fiber? She obviously has the superior intellect and good taste it requires to both handle and prepare us befittingly. She would not leave us abandoned in a drawer rotting away to our death. Oh, please! Move along to the bakery!

Pretending to ignore the jeering, I would quickly grab my baggie full of apples, a bunch of bananas, and an onion (the only produce that would be seen with me) before making my escape to the bakery where all my friends were. Nothing to hide from there.

> **COOKIES AND CAKES:** (*With embarrassingly loud volume*) Girrrrl! Get your fine self on over. We just popped out of the oven. Don't we smell good? Uh-huh. Take a bite. Take another. You come on back around before you leave, now. Ya hear?

Though my trip through the bakery would provide temporary relief, more perils were waiting around every corner. Land mines of confusion and degradation were scattered here and there, mostly via the voices of the products. (Do groceries talk to you?) Well, I would hear things like, "Buy me! I'm fat free," or "No, buy me. I'm *not* fat free." There were products that wanted to jump into my cart and others that turned their faces away at the sight of me.

And of course there were the other shoppers to deal with. Their mouths weren't moving, but boy were they screaming at me.

> **SKINNY MOM WITH THREE KIDS IN CART:** Why, yes, I can eat all of this junk food (*pointing to her*

array of sugary treats and snack items). I have simply been blessed with a high metabolism. It's the best. (*Throws head back and lets out an evil, eat-your-heart-out chuckle.*)

SKINNY MOM WITH ONE KID IN CART: I only buy organics for my family. And I never eat partially hydrogenated oil. Oh, my gosh! Look at all those by-products in your cart. (*Points at my cart with look of horror and hides child's eyes.*) And you wonder why you can't keep weight off?

BATTLEFIELD: CHECKOUT LANE

Okay, okay. So that was bad enough, but the worst was always last. My bruised ego and I would eventually make it through the aisles of the store, but waiting in the checkout lane would be the GGGs: *Grocery Glamour Girls*.

I know you've met them before. They are the women who look so kind from a distance—so well dressed and happy, resting comfortably on the cover of every magazine. They wait until you are adequately trapped in the checkout lane (someone in front of you and someone behind who ain't movin' for nothin'), and then they hoist out their assault rifles (with silencer, of course).

GGG #1: I just had twins a month ago, and my abs are already smooth and tight. See? Look at them. *I said, "Look at them!"* How long has it been since you had your babies? Oh, that's right . . . a couple of years. And your abs? (*Sarcastic clap.*)

GGG #2: Don't you think your husband would be soooo excited if you looked like me in the bedroom? (*Gently caresses her curves.*) You know that's right. (*Snap, snap, snap.*)

GGG #3: Get a clue, lady. I don't understand why you can't take off weight. Everybody knows that a steady diet of water and oxygen is all it takes. You only truly need food every forty days.

The products on the shelves may not talk to you, but I know I'm not alone when it comes to dealing with the GGGs. These gals don't take prisoners. Several studies have been conducted that show a direct relationship between women's (as well as young girls') body dissatisfaction and magazine reading. And what do you think about this? According to statistics released by the American Society for Aesthetic Plastic Surgery, nearly 11.7 million surgical and nonsurgical cosmetic procedures were performed in the US in 2007, a number that is surely much higher now.[4] Do you think that has anything to do with society's readily displayed, unrealistic definition of beauty?

BATTLEFIELD: LIVING ROOM

Close relatives of the GGGs, the TGGs (Television Glamour Girls) waged war against me in my own home. Here's how they roll:

TGG #1: I just lost forty pounds on the Magical System of Wonders. My life is finally worth living! Results may vary, and watch out for the looming possibility of frequent bowel urges that could make everything else in life JUST A BIT awkward.

TGG #2: Thirty pounds ago, my husband was embarrassed to have me on his arm. Now that I've shed those extra pounds with Fat Stalkers, he can't keep his hands off me. I've even seen his friends checking me out! (*Giggles flirtatiously in face of drooling man.*)

Don't let your guard down around these lovely ladies for even one second. The TGGs have enormous influence. Weight loss is a nearly $55 billion a year business, with Americans spending nearly $40 million of that total.[5]

BATTLEFIELD: BEDROOM

Those GGGs and TGGs must have had a time-released messaging ability, because any time romance was in the air I could hear them loud and clear. Visions of their perfectly sculpted rear ends clad in patches of fabric held together by slim strings marched right to the forefront of my mind (a reminder of the miracle-working power of yoga). Immediately following would be the vision of my dimpled thighs rubbing together ever so attractively in my grandma-style swimsuit. How sexy can one woman get?

Of course Bill's body hadn't changed a bit since our honeymoon night. Still firm and toned, he would proudly walk around the room torturing me (not intentionally, mind you) with what I didn't feel I deserved. He would climb into bed, where I was safely hidden beneath a layer of covers and my flannel sleep set, and put his arm around me.

"Oh, Bill, please don't touch my fat," I would say.

"Can't I even hug you?"

Well, okay, I would think. *You can touch my wrists and my ankles, and I think my shoulder blades are still firm. You can touch me there.*

Sounds like the makings of a great love scene, doesn't it?

BATTLEFIELD: FAMILY GATHERINGS

The torment didn't stay tucked away safely in the privacy of my own home. Getting together with extended family took my anxiety to new heights.

When you think of big family get-togethers you probably imagine a menagerie of people: intoxicated uncles, overly affectionate aunts, cheerful grandmas, and the fat cousin. That last one was me. For both my mom and dad's families, weight was always an important and readily discussed issue. Whoever was thinnest or had lost the most weight recently received quite a bit of positive attention. Though I knew I was loved, I had to battle through feeling like I was a disappointment—the cute face with big bones, the granddaughter who couldn't control her portions, the one who had inherited all the bad genes.

Oh, and it was worse with Bill's family. You see, his family members all look like models. In fact, I'm pretty sure his sisters actually *were* models. Tall, thin, elegantly light eaters . . . adjectives wanting nothing to do with me.

BATTLEFIELD: CHURCH

And, no, the battle in my mind did not take Sundays off. In fact, sometimes it got worse. After spending far too much time trying to find a pair of pants that first of all fit me, and then second, didn't accentuate how big my rear end really was, I would put my focus on the Lord and head off to worship. With my heart set on ignoring my own petty frustrations, I would enter the sanctuary with a determined smile.

Then the supernatural would take place: I would somehow be endowed with extra powerful hearing. I'd catch every conversation dealing with weight.

SISTER-IN-CHRIST #1: Oh, my, Gloria. You look amazing! How much weight have you lost? Hey, why don't you sit by me?
SISTER-IN-CHRIST #2: Yeah, Jan, I've found that

when I pray over my pantry, I simply lose the desire to overeat. It's that simple. Praise God!

SISTER-IN-CHRIST #3: And, don't forget . . . our bodies are the temple of the Living God, and God don't want no rundown temple now, right?

I cringe to think of the countless hurting people who sat all around me, many I might have been able to encourage with a simple hello. But because of my preoccupation with the condition of "my temple," those opportunities passed by completely ignored.

BATTLEFIELD: BATHROOM

I'm sure you know personally how difficult the battle can be in the bathroom. There my biggest enemies converged upon me as a team. Reflection and Trainer spent much of their free time sitting on my vanity, where they kept good company with another character—one who wielded immense power over me: the Scale God. First thing every day, I would pay homage to this powerful being through my morning ritual: pee out every drop of liquid I could possibly squeeze from my body, clip my nails, blow my nose, take off all my clothing and jewelry, exhale, and stand before him.

SCALE GOD: You may approach.

FAT CHRISTIAN WOMAN: Thank you, your majesty.

SCALE GOD: What are you here for today?

FAT CHRISTIAN WOMAN: I would like to find out my worth, your majesty.

SCALE GOD: All right then, you may step up.

FAT CHRISTIAN WOMAN: Thank you, sir. (*Holds breath, sucks in stomach, and steps up as lightly as possible.*)

SCALE GOD: I'm afraid you aren't worth anything today. You are up two pounds from yesterday. You may step down. Be gone with you.

I lived for the days when Scale God would tell me I had value. Those were the days when the numbers were down a bit. Trainer would lighten up on me, and my entire outlook on life would change. So would my attitude toward my family and friends. I had a bigger smile for the kids (Bill and I had another two by this time) and a friendlier tone for my husband. Birds and deer would gather around my house in song. Those days were few and far between.

Not seeing the insanity of it all, I continued to bow down to the little white square in my bathroom, seeing it as the key to my contentment and significance. Oh, how I prayed that it would one day display the magic number—a number that would tell me I had arrived. One that would say, "You are now one of the beautiful, the worthy, the victorious."

MEET SABBY

My obvious preoccupation with weight led to another obsession in my life: dieting. Any diet you can think of, I've
probably tried. Anything the TGGs recommended, I did.
I restricted carbs, and I went all carbs. I did liquids, and I
did pills. I even did shots (injections, not tequila). Anything
promising me that I could melt off the pounds.

And I wasted so much money. I purchased videos, club
memberships, mail-delivery food, motivational books, exercise devices of all kinds—you name it. I was desperate for
answers and aching for weight-loss victory.

I'd do okay for a while, even losing a few pounds here
and there. But just as soon as my pants were a bit looser, a
friend would talk me into "rewarding" myself. This friend's
name is Saboteur, but I call her "Sabby." She lives next
door to Reflection and Trainer, and her advice—although
sounding so good at first—usually left me defeated.

SABBY: Oh, Teasi, you've had such a stressful day.
You really should take the kids for ice cream.

FAT CHRISTIAN WOMAN: But, it's not on my diet.
And I've been doing so well.

SABBY: Girl, you know you can get right back on
track tomorrow. Just go this time. You deserve it.
Plus no one can live on that diet forever.

FAT CHRISTIAN WOMAN: I guess you're right. I can
burn it off tomorrow.

Sabby's advice always killed my efforts. The guilt of having blown it just once ignited a full surrender to indulgence. Within days all was lost of my efforts, and the pounds would come back with friends.

NIGHTLY RITUAL

With every failed diet I became more certain that there was something inherently wrong with me. I wondered if there was some sin my ancestors had committed long before that left me cursed. I felt like a fool to my friends and family because I could never seem to follow through on my grand diet plans. And Trainer let me have it just about every night before I fell asleep.

> TRAINER: Okay, Teasi, this is ridiculous. You were doing it for three days and then you totally blew it. Your pants are even tighter on you now than they were before.
>
> FAT CHRISTIAN WOMAN: I know. I'm so sorry. I'll do better tomorrow. In fact, I'm not eating at all until I've lost thirty pounds.

This nightly ritual was insanity. Every night I would make aggressive plans to do better in the morning.

THE BIG DISCONNECT

My failure with weight sent me on many biblical searches. I

tried so hard to find the hidden key in Scripture that would solve my problems and set me on the path to high metabolism heaven. All the while I couldn't help but notice the parts that didn't seem to be working for me. Romans 8:37 told me that through Christ I was more than a conqueror. Really? I couldn't even conquer a diet. Philippians 4:13 told me that I could do all things because Christ would give me the strength. Well, where was He when the Oreos came calling? How could the Maker of Heaven and Earth part the waters of the Red Sea, push down the walls of Jericho, and raise the dead, yet not help me win my war on fat?

And then there were verses I just wanted to ignore. Like the verse that told me I should rejoice when others rejoice (Rom. 12:15). Well, I was rejoicing when they failed. I couldn't help but secretly celebrate when someone I knew had put on a few pounds. After all, I didn't want to be the only fatty in town. (Misery loves company.)

There was an obvious disconnect between what the Bible promised (and required) and what I was experiencing, and that created an increasing desperation in me. I loved God and wanted to live a life that was pleasing to Him, but it seemed no matter how much I studied, prayed, served . . . something was desperately missing.

Dramatically, I poured onto the pages of my journals ridiculous (and pain-filled) plans for how to make my life better.

JOURNAL JOURNEY

June 28, 1997

I'm getting ready to go to sleep feeling overweight and defeated again. I am full of the knowledge of how to get my weight off. I know the key to success is giving my pain to God instead of food. I know I will never be skinny, and that's fine. I don't need to be. I do want to be lean—fit. I want to be at a comfortable weight so that it is no longer an issue that keeps me bound in depression or feeling like a failure. I know what size I should be and can be. I want to be there, and I can do it with God's help and my own. I'm weary of the self-defeating cycle. I want off this horrible ride of falling asleep angry at myself and waking up to do what hurts me most: eating too much of the wrong stuff. Lord, Jesus, I need Your strength and mercy. I need Your forgiveness, and most desperately I need to see myself as You see me so that my focus will be healthy and godly. I don't want to be thinner for vain reasons. I want to feel good about my appearance, but mostly I want to be free of this self-mutilating process I'm in. I know I fall short in so many ways, but I come to You begging for mercy and strength.

Doesn't that journal entry make it sound like I was on the right track? Like I simply wanted to be healthy and see myself through God's eyes? I would *never* want to be skinny for *vain* reasons.

Who did I think I was kidding? Years later I was still singing the same song.

February 13, 2001

I go to bed most every night regretting the eating choices I've made and feeling angry at myself. Then I make grand plans to do better—plans I don't keep. I'm sick of this insanity, but apparently not enough to change it. I really, really, really want to figure out what the heck keeps me in this horrible, self-defeating, hellish cycle. Why am I doing this? Why? Why? I feel like I'm drowning in the insanity of this. I want to be free.

November 16, 2002

Well, here I am again. I want to develop a plan of attack that will help me lose fifteen pounds. I've lost quite a bit, but I need to lose these last few pounds. I need to continue to run five times a week and follow an eating plan correctly 98 percent of the time.

May 20, 2003

Okay, I'm up again (on the scale) and wanting to be healthier and lose some weight. My goal is to lose twenty pounds. I think that would be a good weight for me. I need to set realistic goals. I'm not really sure how to eat. I'm confused, but I do know that I love exercise. So, I'm going to say six days a week I need thirty minutes of aerobics. Then I need to make sure I'm drinking enough water.

April 12, 2005

Well, there are some things I want to do for myself. I don't really know how to make this time different than the rest of my attempts, but I've got to try. I've gotten myself up to a size 16–18. I'm not really happy at this size. I want to be a 12. I know I will feel much more like myself at that size. I think a plan that will be good for me is to walk five days a week for thirty minutes or more and substitute shakes and snack bars for meals.

MISSING THE GOOD STUFF

I prayed for answers. I confessed every sin I could imagine might be responsible for my fat. I asked people about deliverance ministry, thinking that maybe there was a demon responsible for my misery that needed to be sent packing. Sometimes I went to the other extreme and secretly wished for some demon of thinness to possess me. Even if it meant having dark circles under my eyes and spinning my head in true Linda Blair (of *Exorcist* fame) fashion, at least I would be skinny. (Can you believe how crazy it got?) And I fantasized about a day when some well-meaning friend would look me straight in the eyes and say, "Teasi, you really need to eat."

Even more ridiculous is the fact that my obsession with fat and failure robbed me of a lot of the good in my life. On family vacations, on dates with Bill, at parties . . . *everywhere* . . . I was always aware of my weight, and that awareness kept me from truly living.

It did not matter what I might have been doing right. Someone might say, "Teasi, you are such a great mom." But I would immediately think to myself, "Yeah, but I'm fat." Or they'd say, "Thank you so much for your prayers. You are such a great friend." Again I'd think, "Yeah, but I'm fat."

My issue with weight was the undercurrent of my whole life.

LORD, TAKE ME

Whether you think I was crazy or not, I did. And because things never seemed to change for me this side of heaven, I started wanting to cross to the other side. My failures with weight and victorious Christian living left me aching to talk to God face to face. I wanted answers. I wanted relief. I wanted my heavenly body. I wanted it so badly that I spent more time than I should have contemplating death.

I did not want to count my blessings. I did not want to renew my mind. I wanted to get away from myself. I wanted to escape Trainer and Sabby and Reflection. I wanted freedom. I wanted peace. I wanted to drink Clorox and let it take me away. But I couldn't. I didn't want my babies to find me like that.

I would have to continue living, but something had to change. If it couldn't be the size of my hips, then it needed to be something. Anything.

TURNING POINT

I felt miserable and, honestly, quite hopeless. Then something deep inside — some inner mechanism hidden beneath the mountains of self-effort and walls of self-protection — surrendered. I was reduced to the only thing I knew to be true: *I believe there is a God.* It was neither grand in its wording nor magical in any way, but this next journal entry marked a turning point for me — one with significance I would not fully understand for quite some time.

April 10, 2006

I really don't have words, but I'm here again — wanting change — needing freedom and success — lasting success.

I pray today for healing in the deepest recess of my heart and soul — healing in whatever wounded mechanism keeps me defeating myself. I give it to You, Lord. I love You, and that's about all I do know. I have no plan today except to hold desperately to You. I am Yours.

I didn't know it at the time, but I can see now that this was the journal entry God was waiting for. Instead of asking God to help me get skinny, I asked Him for *healing*.

WHAT ABOUT YOU?
WORLDLY DESIRES DIVULGED

1. When you look at the covers of magazines, what kinds of things go through your mind? _____
_____

2. How do you compare yourself to the women on the covers of magazines? _____
_____
_____

3. Do you ever say, "I wish I had _____ like she does?" If so, what is it that you've desired? _____

_____

_____

4. Be really honest now. Do you see your worth or value in terms of these things. For example, do you think you are actually *worth* more when you weigh less? Or do you think you are a more *valuable* person when you have more valuables in your possession? _____

_____

_____

_____

5. What do you think God would say about your last answer?

_____

_____

_____

6. You might not have Sabby (the one who always tries to sidetrack you) in your head, but you probably hear a voice like hers. Have you ever heard anything from her just when you were trying to do something God's way instead of the world's? For example, just as you were trying to love yourself as you are, Sabby might say, "But it wouldn't hurt to just get a few nips and tucks"—setting you right back on vanity's trail. What does she say to you?

a. SABBY: _____

_____

_____

_____

_____

b. YOU: _____

_____

_____

_____

_____

7. Make an honest list of the worldly things you want:

_____

_____

_____

_____

_____

_____

PEP TALK: WE'RE ALL TEMPTED

This world has a lot of tempting things to offer us. Money, looks, clothes, luxury minivans with widescreen TVs and reclining leather seats that swivel all the way around that can be easily stowed below for extra storage space. (Sorry for that little walk down desire lane). The fact is we're all tempted. Jesus was tempted. Temptations are nothing to feel bad about. It's when those temptations become desires that problems arise.

The desires of our hearts can lead us to either life or death. When we start to long for the things of this world, we will always feel disappointed. We aren't made for this world. The world is all about the things that are fading away, and we are made to be all about eternity. Taking an honest look at the things we're longing for is a great step toward realigning our desires before they get the best of us.

FORWARD FOCUS: DESIRES

- Psalm 37:4—Delight yourself also in the LORD, and He shall give you the **desires** of your heart.
- Matthew 16:24—Then Jesus said to His disciples, "If anyone **desires** to come after Me, let him deny himself, and take up his cross, and follow Me.
- Matthew 16:25—For whoever **desires** to save his life will lose it, but whoever loses his life for My sake will find it.
- Mark 4:19—And the cares of this world, the deceitfulness of riches, and the **desires** for other things entering in choke the word, and it becomes unfruitful.

- Mark 10:44—And whoever of you **desires** to be first shall be slave of all.
- Galatians 5:24—And those who are Christ's have crucified the flesh with its passions and **desires**.
- Ephesians 2:3—Among whom also we all once conducted ourselves in the lusts of our flesh, fulfilling the **desires** of the flesh and of the mind, and were by nature children of wrath, just as the others.
- 2 Timothy 4:3—For the time will come when they will not endure sound doctrine, but according to their own **desires**, because they have itching ears, they will heap up for themselves teachers.
- James 1:14—But each one is tempted when he is drawn away by his own **desires** and enticed.
- James 4:1—Where do wars and fights come from among you? Do they not come from your **desires** for pleasure that war in your members?
- Revelation 22:17—And the Spirit and the bride say, "Come!" And let him who hears say, "Come!" And let him who thirsts come. Whoever **desires**, let him take the water of life freely.

FOUR

OPENING A LOCKED HEART

• • •

We all have blind spots, don't we? Things we just don't see?
Sometimes it's a trail of toilet paper stuck to our shoe. Sometimes it's a limited perspective that keeps us a creature of self-
defeating habits. Either way, thank God for people who will
give it to us straight — the ones who, no matter how awkward
it will feel, have the guts to say, "You've got something green
on your tooth." They are the ones who love us enough to save
us from ourselves.

Bill has always been one of those people for me, and back
when I was barely hanging on, his willingness to confront me
saved my life. Having seen all he could of my pain/craziness,
and knowing I desperately needed a mental adjustment, Bill
made the decision to take me to get help. No, he didn't take
me to get a partial lobotomy (though he might have considered it); he took me to . . . a seminar.

I'm sure you can imagine how excited I was for this
opportunity (not!). Actually, it would be an understatement
to say that my heart just wasn't into making this trip. Not only
was I hesitant to leave the kids, but the title of the weekend's

agenda did nothing to entice me: "Experiencing the Father's Embrace." My personal translation of this title was, "Getting a hug from God." Sweet as that sounded, I was desperate, and a hug wasn't going to save me. I needed a mountain-moving miracle. I needed an overdose of hope—some supernatural intervention to keep me living. But Bill was insistent, so we (Bill, me, and old reliable Sabby) loaded up the car bound for Chicago.

IS THIS A JOKE?

After a nearly nine-hour trip, we finally made it to our hotel, which was also the venue of the conference. We were just in time for the first session of the weekend.

Finding our seats, I tucked my Bible under my chair, crossed one leg over the other and my arms across my chest. (My body language expressed my feelings quite well.) My expectations for a good outcome were about as high as a kite still in its wrapper. Bill, on the other hand, was all smiles. So was just about everyone else around me.

The night began with a worship band playing a familiar song. And that's where the familiarity ended. All around me, unexpected displays of joy erupted, startling me out of my futile attempt to block out my surroundings. Sabby was startled too.

SABBY: What on earth? Do you see those kids over there?

FAT CHRISTIAN WOMAN: Yes. I see them.

SABBY: Why are they waving flags around? That is so inappropriate. Where are the parents?

FAT CHRISTIAN WOMAN: I don't know. I didn't know this was a kid event.

SABBY: And look at that woman in front of you. What kind of dancing is that? Where's her pole?

FAT CHRISTIAN WOMAN: I don't know. Just stop looking at her.

I began to have that "We're not in Kansas anymore" feeling and really wanted to bolt. I was used to demonstrative worship at my home church—loud singing and arms raised to God—but I'd never seen this kind of stuff. Thankfully, I can more than appreciate the beauty of diversity in the Body of Christ now, but in that moment I was not in the mood to be tolerant. I didn't want to be stretched.

Just when I was contemplating making a quick getaway, the worship ended and someone took the podium to speak. Everyone sat down, making it impossible for me to slip away unnoticed. So, I looked over at Bill, rolled my eyes so that he'd be sure to see I wasn't amused, and crossed my arms even more tightly across my chest. Nothing was getting in.

Then the speaker was introduced. "Ladies and gentlemen, please welcome Mr. Jack Frost."

SABBY: What? Are you kidding me? Oh, this is rich.

FAT CHRISTIAN WOMAN: Yeah, I agree. I thought we were in Chicago, not the North Pole.

SABBY: Hilarious! Maybe Frosty the Snowman will come out next.

FAT CHRISTIAN WOMAN: All right. Stop. We're not being nice.

SABBY: Seriously, Teasi. This is so stupid. I can't believe Bill, of all people, would bring you here. After this session, you should leave.

FAT CHRISTIAN WOMAN: I was just thinking that myself.

JUST ONE MORE SESSION

Physically trapped, emotionally distraught, and mentally irritated, I sat and listened to Mr. Jack Frost begin his tale. He'd hardly spoken for five minutes when I made up my mind that the next two hours of my life would be a total waste. What could this man—a retired sea captain, of all things—say that could change the course of my life? What could we possibly have in common? It was hopeless.

Because I couldn't leave, I continued to listen. Eventually I had to admit that the man's transparency was keeping a bit of my attention. He was being so honest—revealing things about his own pain and suffering that most people don't usually admit to. He spoke of his abusive and dysfunctional upbringing and how it hurt him. He talked about the mistakes he'd made with his own children and his wife. He confessed his pride and arrogance. He put it all on the table.

And then he talked about the Father's embrace—that "sweet little hug from God" I thought this conference was all about. Only the embrace *he* described was far more than a simple hug. It was a life-altering power that had transformed every part of Jack Frost's existence. It was the mother of all paradigm shifts that reset the course of his life. It was the mountain-moving miracle for which I was so desperate. He had my full attention.

Two hours passed by much more quickly than I thought it would, and once Mr. Frost concluded the session, he opened up the night for prayer. First he prayed for everyone corporately—a prayer filled with so much love and understanding that almost immediately people all around the room began to cry. I could tell hearts were being touched in significant ways. It seemed that God was speaking to nearly everyone around me. These people were getting what they came for: healing, love, and a touch from God. But I was feeling nothing.

Oh, how I wanted to experience something—a sensation that would prove to me God was aware of *my* pain. I looked at Bill and asked—no, *implored*—"Why don't I feel anything? Where is God for *me*?"

Desperate to get me help, Bill approached Mr. Jack Frost himself and asked him to come pray for me personally.

I was hurting too much to be embarrassed when the man finally made it to me. If this is what it would take to get God's full attention, then by all means bring Jack Frost on over!

Bill gave a quick explanation of my situation while Mr. Frost sat there calmly. I felt certain he would lay hands on me immediately once he heard of my excruciating emotional pain, but he just sat there listening. No look of concern. No bewildered exclamation of, "Oh, my, child . . . how have you made it this far in life?" Nope. Just a steady expression of peace and a simple prayer.

As he prayed I kept waiting for it—waiting for the sensation of power to flood through my body. Waiting for my pulse to quicken. Waiting to lose consciousness. Waiting for . . . well, anything different. But, nothing came. Nothing.

Far beyond worrying that I might hurt the man's feelings, I let him have it. "I am feeling nothing!" I said. "I don't get it. Why don't I feel anything? The prayer is not working."

I thought for sure he was going to tell me that I wasn't feeling anything because I was desperately lost. That mine was a case like none other, and that there truly was no hope for me. But that's not what he said. Although what he did say wasn't much better, it got me thinking. He simply said, "It doesn't matter if you feel it or not. The truth is still the truth." He added, "Some people run into the deep end of the water and dive in head first. Others wade in slowly. But everyone gets in."

After delivering his disappointingly ambiguous message,

he patted my shoulder and stood to walk away. Still no change—well, maybe just one. I decided I would come back for another session.

WHAT YOU LEAST EXPECT

There is an Old Testament story about a mighty warrior named Naaman. He is the captain of the army of the King of Syria, and he is considered a very honorable man. In fact, Scripture says that the Lord used this man to deliver Syria from the hand of its enemies. But there is a big problem with him: he has leprosy.

One day, Naaman gets word via an Israelite servant girl that there is someone back in Israel who can heal him of his disease. When given permission to go on this journey, Naaman heads straight to the King of Israel himself for his healing. The king is disturbed by the request, to put it lightly. In fact, the Bible says the king tears his clothes and says some crazy stuff. But nearby the prophet Elisha is listening, and he tells the king to calm down. "Send the guy to me," he says (in more elegant words, of course). "I'll show him that there's a prophet in Israel."

What does this have to do with anything, you're wondering? Well, keep reading. It's good.

So, Naaman makes his way to Elisha the prophet, expecting him to wave his arms over his leprosy in some magical and extremely spiritual display of power and healing. What happens instead is Elisha tells him to go and wash himself in the Jordan River (a very dirty river, mind you) seven times. That, he tells Naaman, will do the trick.

Naaman is outraged. There were much cleaner rivers back in his hometown. This is a joke—a ridiculous joke meant to make him look like a fool. He isn't going for it. That is, until some of his servants talk some sense into him. They confront him with an ugly truth: Naaman would have done anything he was told as long as it was something *great* and *mighty*. Why is he so hesitant to simply get in the river seven times? Is it because the cure doesn't look the way he wanted it to? Because it didn't appear significant to him?

Thankfully for Naaman, he listens to his friends and realizes his folly. Once he obeys and gets into that muddy river seven times, he is healed immediately. His life is forever changed.

I tell you this story because it describes my experience in Chicago so perfectly. When I walked into that first session, I felt like Bill had taken me to a dirty river. I wanted to leave— to head back home to familiar waters. This trip seemed like such a long way to travel for something so . . . so lackluster and disappointing. But I can't even imagine where I would be now if I hadn't gone . . . and made the decision to stay.

By the time we left that weekend, God had begun a work in me that changed my life completely. God used Jack Frost—the hardened sea captain gone transparent—and his ministry of the Father's love, to save my life.

WHAT ABOUT YOU?
FICKLE FEELINGS

1. Make a list of as many feelings as you can think of (such as joy, fear, embarrassment, excitement, etc.): _____
   _____
   _____
   _____
   _____

2. Look at the list you made in question one. Which of those feelings is your favorite? _____
   _____

3. Which feeling is your least favorite? _____
   _____

4. When you feel the feeling you mentioned in question three, what do you usually do about it (such as chocolate therapy)? _____
   _____
   _____

5. How does doing what you do in number four make you feel? _____
   _____
   _____

6. How does this become a never-ending cycle? _____
_____
_____

7. Do you think it's good for us to base our decisions on our feelings? Why or why not? _____
_____
_____
_____

9. How have your feelings ever misled you? _____
_____
_____

10. How do you think God can use our feelings for His purposes? _____
_____
_____

PEP TALK: GOD CREATED US WITH FEELINGS

Sometimes feelings can be a real frustration. I can't even recall the number of times I've said, "I hate the way I feel today." Mix in hormonal fluctuations, and it can get really ugly fast. But, God actually made us with feelings, and I believe He uses them for His purposes when we submit to Him.

I once heard it said that our feelings are like the indicator lights on the dashboard of a car. Just as the "check oil" light warns us that something needs attention in our engine, a feeling of frustration can warn us that something needs attention in our hearts. I think the goal is to accept that we have a myriad of feelings, and we should thank God for them. But we also need to know that sometimes they are misleading. We must pray for the Holy Spirit's wisdom in order to accurately interpret and act upon what we feel.

FORWARD FOCUS: WISDOM

- Psalm 51:6 — Behold, You desire truth in the inward parts, and in the hidden part You will make me to know **wisdom**.
- Psalm 111:10 — The fear of the LORD is the beginning of **wisdom**; a good understanding have all those who do His commandments. His praise endures forever.
- Proverbs 2:6 — For the LORD gives **wisdom**; from His mouth come knowledge and understanding.
- Proverbs 3:13 — Happy is the man who finds **wisdom**, and the man who gains understanding.
- Isaiah 33:6 — **Wisdom** and knowledge will be the stability of your times, and the strength of salvation.
- Ephesians 1:17 — That the God of our Lord Jesus Christ,

the Father of glory, may give to you the spirit of **wisdom** and revelation in the knowledge of Him.

- Colossians 1:9—For this reason we also, since the day we heard it, do not cease to pray for you, and to ask that you may be filled with the knowledge of His will in all **wisdom** and spiritual understanding.

- Colossians 3:16—Let the word of Christ dwell in you richly in all **wisdom**, teaching and admonishing one another in psalms and hymns and spiritual songs, singing with grace in your hearts to the Lord.

- James 1:5—If any of you lacks **wisdom**, let him ask of God, who gives to all liberally and without reproach, and it will be given to him.

FIVE

NO MORE MISSING OUT

• • •

It can happen anywhere at any time: the moment when we see something we've never seen before—a breakthrough that changes our lives. Your moment could come as you look out over the ocean on a family vacation. It could happen as you stand over the kitchen sink, hands covered in dish soap. It could happen during a worship service or while reading a good book. For me, it happened at that Chicago conference.

Since that time, it seems like one spiritual light switch after another has flipped on for me, revealing all the good stuff God had waiting all along—everything He knew I would need to make it through this life. The Bible says that God has already given you and me *everything* we need to live our lives—physically, emotionally, and spiritually (2 Pet. 1:3). So, if we already have what we need, life really becomes a great "unpacking" of it all. Rather than asking God to give us more, our prayer changes instead to "Help me uncover what you've given me."

For me, the uncovering began when I took a deeper look at something I thought I already had a pretty firm grasp on: Jesus and His relationship with His Father, Almighty God. I knew that Jesus and God had a close relationship. I knew that God couldn't have asked for a better Son (He was sinless after all), and that He was willing to sacrifice that perfect Son to pay the price for my sins. But there was something I had somehow missed, despite all my years of studying the Bible. Something Jesus was trying to show me—to show us—about the beauty and the full power found in that divine relationship.

WWJFO

From an early age, Jesus was aware of the special connection he had with his Dad. We all remember the scene in Luke's gospel in which Mary and Joseph realize after a three-day journey that they've left Jesus behind in Jerusalem. When they return to find Him, Jesus (twelve years old at the time) is sitting in the temple having deep conversations with the teachers. Mary essentially asks him, "Young man, what do you think you're doing?" and Jesus says, "Why did you seek Me? Did you not know that I must be about My Father's business?" (Luke 2:49). The business He's talking about here isn't Joseph's carpentry work. Jesus is talking about the work of His heavenly Father.

And Jesus went on from that time always living to do His heavenly Father's business and only His business. Look at what He says in John 8:28: "When you lift up the Son of

Man, then you will know that I am He, and that I do nothing of Myself; but as My Father taught Me, I speak these things."

Jesus did *nothing* but what His Father showed Him to do. His focus was constantly on His Father, and I believe it's important for us to see this. It makes me think of those WWJD (What Would Jesus Do?) bracelets. I almost wonder if there should be a different one: WWJFO (What Would Jesus Focus On?). After all, His focus is what led to everything He did. His actions all flowed out of His perfect relationship with His Father—a relationship He desperately wants us to have as well.

FOLLOW THE LEADER

Several times in the Bible we see Jesus saying, "Follow Me." In the fourth chapter of Matthew, Jesus asks Peter, Andrew, James, and John all to drop what they are doing to follow Him. At this point, Jesus is asking them to come along on a physical journey—to witness His power and ministry on earth. (And boy, what an incredible eyeful they got!) But not much later, Jesus makes the same request with an interesting twist.

In John 21:19, Jesus is talking with Peter once again by the Sea of Galilee. He says to Peter, "Follow me." He says it again in verse 22. Now remember, by this time Peter has already been following Jesus for quite some time. Why does Jesus keep saying this? I believe the answer can be found a few verses earlier (verse 14): "This is now the third time Jesus showed Himself to His disciples after He was raised from the dead."

Look at the timing here. On this occasion, Jesus is asking Peter to follow him *after He was raised from the dead*. His earthly ministry is pretty much over. Jesus is about to go back to heaven. Why is He still asking Peter to follow? Where is Jesus going that He would continue to repeat this request? Well, here's what Jesus says:

> "Let not your heart be troubled; you believe in God, believe also in Me. In My Father's house are many mansions; if it were not so, I would have told you. I go to prepare a place for you. And if I go and prepare a place for you, I will come again and receive you to Myself; that where I am, there you may be also. And where I go you know, and the way you know." Thomas said to Him, "Lord, we do not know where You are going, and how can we know the way?" Jesus said to him, "I am the way, the truth, and the life. No one comes to the Father except through Me." (John 14:1–6)

From these verses we can see that the journey has changed from the physical to the sacred. Jesus is now asking Peter (and us) to follow Him not just around town, but to the *Father*. And not only does Jesus ask us to follow, but He says

He is *the way*. What is the use of a "way" if there is no destination? But there is a destination, and it appears that leading us to that place is a primary objective for Jesus. His hope was not simply that we would *do* what He *did*, but that we would *go* where He *went*—into the arms of His Father.

If we stop short by following Jesus only as far as salvation from hell, we are stopping far short of everything He died to accomplish.

MEET MY MIGHTY COUNSELOR

So, do you feel like you've followed Jesus all the way to the Father? When you get really honest, would you say that your relationship with God the Father is all it was meant to be? For many years I thought mine was. I was very aware that God loved me, and I wanted everyone else to know that He loved them too. In fact, I believed I was experiencing all the love God had to give me. But I wasn't, and chances are you're not either.

Here's a quick test for you. Without giving it much thought at all, what are the first few words that come to your mind when I say the name "Jesus"? For many years, my list would have looked like this: savior, humble, lover of sinners, sacrifice, healer, gentle, lover of children. Now, what words do you think of when I say "Holy Spirit"? My list would include such things as comforter, counselor, and loving teacher.

Okay, here's the big one. What words first come to your mind when I say "God the Father"? Honestly, my list would include words such as judge, ruler, holy, discipline, chastening, hater of sin, fear. Is your list similar?

The list of words I related to the Father was far different from those I used to describe Jesus and the Holy Spirit. It's quite obvious that my feelings toward the Father were a bit colder and less personal. Why? The answer started to come for me during one of my "sessions" with my Mighty Counselor (a.k.a. the Holy Spirit).

MIGHTY COUNSELOR: Teasi, I want you to think about your attitude.

FAT CHRISTIAN WOMAN: Oh, yeah. I know it's bad. It always has been.

MIGHTY COUNSELOR: Tell me what you remember about your attitude as a young girl.

FAT CHRISTIAN WOMAN: Well, I remember that I was always kind of negative—pouting about this and that—and I was really quite lazy.

MIGHTY COUNSELOR: What did your parents do about it?

FAT CHRISTIAN WOMAN: They were always trying to teach me the importance of having a good attitude. Almost any time I was grounded it was because of my attitude. In fact, I remember my mom saying this quite often: "You're grounded until your attitude changes or Christ returns—whichever comes first." Of course I sat there waiting for the Rapture.

MIGHTY COUNSELOR: So, when your attitude was bad, you were sent away to be alone? You were separated from fellowship with your family for a while, and you purposely kept yourself away from them, right?

FAT CHRISTIAN WOMAN: Yep.

MIGHTY COUNSELOR: Tell me . . . do you think your heavenly Father is upset about your attitude?

FAT CHRISTIAN WOMAN: Of course. I can't ever seem to get it right.

MIGHTY COUNSELOR: So, do you think He has "grounded" you? And are you keeping yourself from Him because of it?

FAT CHRISTIAN WOMAN: (*Long silence.*) Well, yes . . . I guess I am.

This conversation may appear less than epic, but it was a major light-switch moment for me. The issue of my attitude was huge. I had been feeling guilty about it from my earliest years all the way into my adult life. Without being consciously aware, I was living my life like God the Father was disappointed with me—like I was constantly on restriction. My time with the Mighty Counselor showed me that under it all, I believed God was waiting on me to get my attitude right so He could *finally* bless me. And I didn't think it would ever happen because I was a hopeless case.

But, the Bible doesn't say that.

It doesn't say anywhere that God is waiting on us to get our attitude just right before He can bless us. His blessings are based on *His* goodness, not our own. This lie I believed — this misperception I had of the Father's heart — kept me from fully experiencing all the love He was desperately longing to give me. In effect, I was refusing it because I didn't believe I deserved it.

WHAT'S YOUR PROBLEM?

In her book, *Hurt People Hurt People*, Dr. Sandra Wilson says it well: "We all read and interpret the Bible through the defective lens of personal experience."[6] And I would add that we also view our relationship with our heavenly Father through those glasses — glasses muddied by our experiences with our parents and other relationships here on earth.

As crazy as it may seem, even something as simple as my parents teaching me the importance of having a good attitude became a roadblock in my adult life. A good lesson became twisted into a lie I believed for years. Without knowing I had done so, I turned God into my heavenly Disciplinarian. And this kept me from experiencing Him as He *really is*.

Now, if this could happen to me, do you think it's possible it could have happened to you? Is there a personal experience you had as a child (or some other time in your life) that could be creating a roadblock today?

Think about this: What if as you were growing up, your

father was the authoritarian type? Each day he came home from work tired and irritated. He wanted dinner on the table immediately, and he wanted his children to be seen and not heard. He expected immediate obedience and tolerated no silliness. If you were brave enough to discuss your life at the table, you'd better have been sure it was something worth listening to. It better have been good—good grades, awards won. After all, he worked hard to afford you all the privileges you had. If you didn't live up to it, you were not being very appreciative.

Fast forward to your adult life. How are things now? Can you look back and see that you've been living your entire life trying to please your earthly father because when you do well he is happy, and when you fail he withdraws his love. Are you doing that now for God? Do you volunteer for everything at church because you want to be a good girl? Do you feel like you should pray more, study more, or do more and more to please Him? Do you think you have to earn God's love through performance just like you did your earthly dad? If so, you are missing out.

Or maybe your father was passive. He was present at home and didn't demand much; in fact he didn't seem to want anything. He would come home from work, sit in front of the TV for hours, eating dinner in the living room so he wouldn't miss the big game. When you walked in, he would give you a quick smile and a pat on the head, but would not have time to engage in conversation with you. Mom would do all of that. His job was to provide the money for necessities, nothing more. He was there, but he wasn't.

As an adult do you keep your relationship with Father God distant—logical and intellectual and only that? Do you keep your heart to yourself because you don't believe your heavenly Father cares about it just as your earthly father didn't? Do you believe in the Bible, but shy away from any emotional manifestations of God's love? Are you uncomfortable with others around you showing emotion in their relationship with Him? Are you uncomfortable with love in general? If so, you are missing out.

Or maybe your father was directly abusive to you in some way, and if so, you were definitely not alone. There are more than three million reports of child abuse in America each year with over 68 percent of those being sexual abuse by a family member.[7] If this was your story, you were probably desperate for your daddy's love. When you heard his car pull up, your heart skipped a beat because you were excited to see him. Only when he came in the door he was drunk. He would immediately yell at your mom and push your little sister aside as if she were an annoying piece of furniture in his way. But sometimes he was sober, and you lived for those moments because he would hold you in his lap. You were so happy to have his attention that you chose to ignore where his hands traveled, and you would never tell anyone about that because you were afraid to make him mad.

So as an adult you are left with this strange mix of emotions. You want to love God, but how can you possibly call God your Father? How can you trust your heart to Him? Every time you trusted in your past, you were hurt. Daddy was unpredictable and became one to be feared, not held by. Do you resist God's touch now? Do you believe that He is someone everyone else can trust, but not you? Do you hold back your heart from Him because you just can't stand to be hurt again? If so, you are missing out.

FALSE ACCUSATIONS

The point of taking a look at our relationships with our parents, and even more specifically our fathers, is not to build a case for blame. Blaming others doesn't get us anywhere. The point is to begin to identify potential false accusations we've piled up against God. Have we given him a false rap sheet, of sorts? Does our list of adjectives describe the true nature and heart of our heavenly Father?

The only way we can find out is to look at what the Bible says about His heart. And one amazingly simple way to find out a ton about our heavenly Dad is to look at the life of Jesus.

Now, remember all those warm fuzzy feelings we had about Jesus when we made our list of descriptions for Him? We think of Jesus as someone we are very comfortable with. We might even see Him as our big brother who protects us from angry Dad when we've blown it.

But take a look at what Jesus had to say about Himself.

"If you had known Me, you would have known My Father also; and from now on you know Him and have seen Him." Philip said to Him, "Lord, show us the Father, and it is sufficient for us." Jesus said to him, "Have I been with you so long, and yet you have not known Me, Philip? He who has seen Me has seen the Father; so how can you say, 'Show us the Father'?" (John 14:7–9)

On many other occasions, Jesus tells us that when we've seen Him, we've seen the Father. So, if we look at the character and heart of Jesus, we've actually seen the character and heart of the Father.

What do we see in Jesus? We see Him healing the hurting and the sick. We see Him giving sight to the blind. We see Him taking time to talk to harlots and tax collectors. We see Him angry at the self-righteous and religious folks who thought their actions were winning them heavenly brownie points.

And we see Him being a servant.

Jesus, knowing that the Father had given all things into His hands, and that He had come from God and was going to God, rose from supper and laid aside His garments, took a towel and girded Himself. After that, He poured water into a basin and began to wash the disciples' feet, and to wipe

them with the towel with which He was girded.
(John 13: 3–5)

Jesus got down on his knees and washed the filth off the feet of his disciples. He performed a job that was normally reserved for the lowliest of servants in those days—washing feet that would have been covered with dirt and potentially animal feces (remember the mode of transportation in that day). He humbled Himself before them, and when He did, He showed us the Father.

As you read this scene from the life of our Savior—the One who came to show us the heart of His Father and bring us into His arms—imagine something. Take the disciples out of that chair and put yourself in their place. Now, picture your heavenly Father at your feet. See His eyes filled with nothing but adoration looking up into yours. Hear Him asking, "My sweet, sweet girl. May I please wash your feet? May I wash away the filth and the pain of this world that has piled up on you and left you feeling dirty? May I serve *you*, My daughter? Please let Me."

I don't know about you, but I can love a Daddy like that. In fact, I want nothing more than to love Him. And now I know in order to do that, I must first receive *all* that He's offering me. I must first allow Him to make right all the wrongs I have believed about Him. I must allow truth to tear down the wall of lies so that the good stuff can get in. It is as

Scripture says, "We love Him because He first loved us" (1 John 4:19).

A PLEA TO KNOW YOU, FATHER

Precious Heavenly Father,

I can't believe how I have misjudged You. All these years, the lies I have believed about Your true heart have kept me from feeling the unconditional love You have desired to give. Please forgive me for that. I did not understand the truth, but now I am beginning to see.

Please continue to open my eyes to the ways I have misperceived You. I want to trust you completely and to experience Your love. Fill me from head to toe.

From this day forward, I put on new glasses. I want to see clearly. I want to know You more. When I read my Bible now, it won't be out of religious duty, but out of desire to find out about who You are — to read about how much You adore me. I want to know everything about You.

Please fill my heart so full of Your love that all other healing You want to do can occur. I understand that I cannot love myself or anyone else until I am first filled with Your love for me. I accept that and embrace that truth.

Thank you, precious Lord Jesus, for showing me the heart of the Father in all that You did while You were on earth. Thank You for being the Way to Him. Thank You for showing me how to climb back into my Daddy's lap. Thank You for dying for my sins — for all that You did to make this relationship possible for me.

I love You. I embrace the life You have for me. I embrace change.
I embrace healing. I embrace Father God.

In Jesus' name,

Amen

WHAT ABOUT YOU?
MISPERCEPTIONS UNMASKED

1. List three adjectives that would describe your dad while you were growing up:

    a. _____

    b. _____

    c. _____

2. List three adjectives that would describe your mom while you were growing up:

    a. _____

    b. _____

    c. _____

3. Be honest here: How would you describe the way they felt about you when you were a child? For example, did you feel like they adored you, or did you feel like you were a bother, or somewhere in between? _____

    _____

    _____

    _____

4. Looking at your responses to the first three questions, how do you think the way you felt about your parents and perceived how they felt toward you has transferred over into your relationship with God? In other words, how has it affected the way you would describe Him, and the way you think He feels toward you? _____

_____

_____

_____

_____

5. Pray and ask the Mighty Counselor (Holy Spirit) to bring to mind any potential stowaways you might have brought with you from childhood into your adult life. Are there attitudes or behaviors you've ascribed to your heavenly Father simply because they existed in your earthly parents? What is the Mighty Counselor hoping for you to see? What would you say to Him?

    a. **MIGHTY COUNSELOR:** _____

_____

_____

_____

    b. **YOU:** _____

_____

_____

_____

6. How could having a more correct understanding of the nature and heart of your heavenly Father change your life?_____

_____

_____

_____

_____

_____

_____

PEP TALK: GET TO KNOW YOUR DADDY

It was so very important to Jesus that we know His Father (who happens to be our Father too). As Christians, it is essential that we see the Father for who He really is. No matter how good our earthly parents are, He is far better. We can't settle for seeing Father God as just a bigger (and more demanding) version of our parents. If we do, we'll miss out on parts of what He wants for us.

Even though it can be hard, we've got to take our hands out of our earthly parents' hands, so to speak, and put them into God's. He wants to parent us now . . . His way. The Holy Spirit helps us make the full transition by showing us what's getting in the way, if we let Him.

FORWARD FOCUS: THE FATHER IS LOVE

- 1 John 4:8 — He who does not love does not know God, for God is **love**.

God defines Himself as love. To see a bit more of the true nature of our heavenly Father, replace the word "love" with the words "the Father" in the following verses:

- 1 Corinthians 13:4–8 — **Love** (the Father) suffers long and is kind; **love** does not envy; **love** does not parade itself, is not puffed up; does not behave rudely, does not seek its own, is not provoked, thinks no evil; does not rejoice in iniquity, but rejoices in the truth; bears all things, believes all things, hopes all things, endures all things. Love never fails.

SIX

NO MORE ORPHAN LIVING

●●●

One friend comes and takes my doll, cheerfully sitting to play
My heart rate soars, my stomach's a knot
Hey! That belongs to me.
Another comes and takes my role, making the audience laugh
The tears roll down, my stomach's a knot
Hey! That belongs to me.
Again one comes and takes the guys, walking around so thin
The anger builds, my stomach's a knot
Hey! That belongs to me.
Another friend comes and takes the stage
Teaching the Word of God
Hopelessness invades, my stomach's a knot
Hey! That belongs to me.
The Father comes and takes my heart
Gently pouring in His love
Jealousy leaves, inheritance comes
Yes! That belongs to me.

Do you ever want to call one of your childhood friends simply to apologize for what a crazy nut you were back in the day? Perhaps you're haunted by the memory of that horrific sleepover—the one where you joined in on pouring warm water over your best friend's hand while she slept just to see if she would wet herself. Or maybe you're embarrassed about that "Truth or Dare" game gone terribly wrong.

Well, I know the feeling. In fact, I have apologized to my childhood friends many times. You see, I didn't realize it then, but I was a very difficult friend to have. Of course, I saw myself as an incredibly loyal friend, one who would never leave your side. But, that was the problem: I would *never* leave your side! I was extremely possessive of my friends— or I should say "friend," because I only had one at a time. After all, how can a girl be completely devoted to more than that?

Now, even though I was perfectly content to have my *one best friend*, sometimes she would decide to play with someone besides me. It was not pretty when that occurred.

YOUNG FAT GIRL: Hey, Christina! Do you want to spend the night tonight?

FRIEND: Well, I do, but I'm spending the night with Lee Anne tonight. Maybe tomorrow.

SABBY: What did she just say to you?

YOUNG FAT GIRL: She's spending the night with Lee Anne. (*Increased heart rate.*)

SABBY: How can she do that? How can she turn her back on you like that?

YOUNG FAT GIRL: I don't know. (*Tears welling up in eyes.*)

SABBY: You would NEVER spend the night with anyone but her. I can't believe she's doing this to you. I don't think you should EVER talk to her again. That will show her.

YOUNG FAT GIRL: You're right! I would never do that to her. Never! How can she call herself my friend?

Scenes like this happened many times in my early childhood, and, sadly enough, they carried on through the years. I can remember feeling betrayed when my *one* high school friend dared to go off without me. And I can remember feeling the same way about my *one* friend in college. (Can we say *weirdo*?)

What's really sad is that I knew how unhealthy my behavior was. I understood that it was normal for people to have several good friends at a time, but I couldn't stop my possessive and jealous behavior. And it didn't stop when I became a Christian, either, which only made the inner turmoil greater. It was very clear to me that God did not approve of jealousy. I knew He did not want me to be irrationally angry about what my friends had going on in their lives, but no matter how hard I tried to act better, I just couldn't. The pain and shame would turn into a big self-pity cycle, which would make me an even more difficult friend to deal with.

Thankfully, I am no longer possessive with my friends, and in fact, I have several healthy friendships (at the same time!). I have also been forgiven by all of my victims . . . um, I mean, *friends*. And I have not only gotten over the embarrassment but, as a result of uncovering more of that good stuff God has already given me, I have forgiven myself for being such a jerk. Another divine light switch was flipped on for me, helping me to understand my actions. I see now that they were merely symptoms of a much bigger problem—a problem I believe we all have to deal with: living with an orphan heart.

THE ORPHAN WAY

I read an interesting story once about a little orphan boy who was adopted at around seven years old. The couple who adopted him had prayed for years that God would show them the perfect boy, and they were thrilled when the day finally came that they could call that boy their son.

The couple gave the boy everything. They gave him a wonderful room to call his own. They gave him new clothes and toys. They gave him all the love they had to give. They absolutely adored him. But even though he had been given all of these things—even though he was now truly part of a family—he couldn't completely accept it.

The boy couldn't keep himself from folding a few extra dinner rolls into his napkin to hide in his bedroom. He couldn't stop burying his favorite toys in a secret place deep within his closet. He couldn't stop wondering when everything would be taken away from him. He couldn't help it because he couldn't let go of *the orphan way.*

ORPHANED IN THE GARDEN

Now, most of us would think that the orphan way is only experienced by children who have lost their parents. So, if I were to say that I believe we are all—in one way or another—orphans, your first reaction might be to disagree if you were raised by your parents. But, the word *orphan* can have a much broader meaning. It can refer to a person or thing that is without protective covering. And in the Greek, *orphan* can mean one who is *comfortless.*

Even with the broader definition in mind, you might still think you don't deal with orphan issues in your life. But let me point out one interesting thing. According to traditional Christian theology, we are all born "without protective affiliation." In other words, we are born alienated from God (our Protector) thanks to our ancestors, Adam and Eve. Back in Genesis, when the first man and woman disobeyed God by eating that dumb apple, they were sent out of the garden of Eden. They experienced a spiritual death (just as they'd been warned)—a separation from the perfect love and intimacy they had always known in the garden. They were homeless. No more security. No safe place. No protective affiliation. They were on their own. They were orphans.

And, as Jack Frost says in his book *Spiritual Slavery to Spiritual Sonship*, "As a result of their [Adam and Eve's] fall, their orphan heart passed down to every succeeding generation, thus becoming the common heritage of all humanity."[8] We retain that heritage—an orphan heart—until we finally learn how to exchange it for a new one. But, that's much easier said than done. For just like the little orphan boy in the example above, even after being brought into a family—the family of God—it is hard for us to abandon our old orphan ways.

MY ORPHAN WAYS

I'd like to take a moment here to tell you about some of my former orphan ways—ways that continued well into my life as a Christian. I'll admit that some of them are embarrassing now that my heart has been changed. But, if we're all gonna get honest here, someone's gotta go first. It might as well be me. I'll start with the biggest one: my bottomless need for approval.

Before I was finally able to receive lasting love and approval from my heavenly Father, I was desperate to get it from people. Nearly everything I did was motivated by that need. Of course I wasn't consciously aware of it at the time, but when I offered to help a friend with her children, I didn't really *want* to help her. I *needed* her to think that I was a great friend. When I signed up to help with this or that at church, I didn't do it because I really *wanted* to do that task, it was because I *needed* someone to think I was such an amazing servant. I *needed* to be counted as one of the spiritually mature—those who sacrifice their time and resources for others. I *needed* to be seen as "someone" because deep inside I didn't really believe I was.

That need for approval went hand-in-hand with another of my orphan ways: competition and jealousy toward others. Because I needed approval so badly, when others around me got it, I was jealous. I couldn't rejoice when others were promoted because inside I was thinking, "Hey, I've been here longer than she has! What's the deal?" When someone was honored at church for starting some amazing new ministry, I'd be trapped in bitterness because it should have been me.

And that disappointment led to another orphan way: hopelessness. When others around me were being blessed or promoted in their jobs or ministries, I couldn't help but feel like nothing good was ever going to happen to me. It seemed like God wanted to give good things to everyone around me, but for me, life was going to be about striving for what little I could get.

YOUR ORPHAN WAYS

So, what about you? Do you think you might have some orphan ways keeping you from living the way God really wants? In appendix A of this book, there is a list of orphan heart tendencies, but one simple way to find out is to answer this question honestly: can you really rejoice when others rejoice? Now I mean *really*. Even more specifically, do you think nothing but happy thoughts when someone gets *exactly* what you've wanted for years, but you don't? Could you say you're not a bit jealous when they get that job you've been dreaming of? That guy you've imagined on *your* arm? That ministry you've always thought was God's call on *your* life? The thing you've been praying about for years?

I'll tell you this: about the only thing that would keep you from being truly happy for others is fearing that nothing good will ever come to you. And that, my friend, is orphan thinking. That is the belief that you have no inheritance. No exciting destiny. And this way of thinking makes it impossible for us to be effective Christians. You know why? Because the Bible says that people will know we are Christians by our love for one another (John 13:35). And if we can't rejoice for each other, we don't have love.

And not only that, but this way of thinking means we can't really love God because we'll always think He's holding out on us. And we won't see Him as a loving Father longing to give us good things. He will be seen only as a master — someone to be served and rarely appeased.

THE DAUGHTER WAY

Now, the opposite of living the orphan way is living the daughter way — living like we belong to a family — like we have a Father—like we're safe. This way is easier to describe than it is to live, simply because it requires letting go of bad habits. Not only bad habits, but we need to let go of lies we've believed about our own identity and about Father God's. Living the daughter way requires us to relinquish our orphan ways, and crazy as it may seem, many of those ways die hard. Without us realizing it, they became our identity—such a huge part of our being—and letting go can be painful.

But it's so worth it, for there is nothing—I mean nothing—like the freedom and peace that a daughter feels.

So, what does the daughter way look like? Here's a glimpse:

- loving people with no strings attached
- loving God simply because He's our Dad, and not for the things He can give us
- believing we have an awesome inheritance instead of feeling the need to fight for anything we can get
- serving God and others because we can't keep ourselves from sharing the love instead of doing it to impress people
- knowing we have value and worth instead of listening to the lies of the devil
- living free and fruitful instead of bound and broken

Take it from this former orphan girl: I don't ever want to go back.

NOT LEFT AS ORPHANS

The good news is Jesus knows our predicament, and He addresses it in the Bible. In John 14:18, He says, "I will not leave you orphans; I will come to you." In this verse "orphans" means more specifically "comfortless and fatherless." And Jesus doesn't leave us that way. Remember that He came to be "the Way" back to the Father. When we follow Him into the embrace of our heavenly Father, the fact is we are not fatherless. And He also comes to us, as He says He will, through the power of the "Helper" or "Comforter" (the Holy Spirit, John 14:16). The truth is we are not comfortless.

We also know we are not orphans because the Bible tells us we've been adopted:

> For you did not receive the spirit of bondage again to fear, but you received the Spirit of adoption by whom we cry out, 'Abba, Father.' The Spirit Himself bears witness with our spirit that we are children of God. (Romans 8:15–16)

We are daughters of the King of Kings, and not only that, but we have been given an inheritance. In fact, we are joint heirs with Jesus (Rom. 8:17). We have the same Father He has, and remember Jesus was all He was because of the Father

He had. Just think about all we could be if we put an end to our orphan thinking and take our rightful place—a place that Jesus prepared for us. It's ours for the taking.

FIRST STEPS

As I said earlier, our orphan ways sometimes die hard. Some of those bad boys have been beating us up for years, and they don't want to leave without a fight. But, if we want to make the truth of our biblical *position* become our actual *experience*, we must show up for the battle.

I'd like to tell you the "three easy ways to slay the orphan in you," but they don't exist. This battle we face is really an individual journey—one that must be made with the Mighty Counselor.

But there are things we can do. We can admit the orphan ways we see in our lives instead of ignoring them. We can turn our focus toward receiving the Father's love, which includes turning our focus away from what our earthly parents might have done wrong and letting them off the hook. And we can make a firm choice (one we declare to all who will hear) to live as daughters and not orphans—accepting the full privilege, blessing, and inheritance that come from that position.

We can also ask God to forgive us for the sinful ways we've acted because of our orphan heart. That sin acts as a barrier keeping us from God, and we want to knock it down. The humility it takes to get that honest with ourselves and with God isn't for sissies.

THE SUPERNATURAL STUFF

Now, we can't do the big stuff—the supernatural stuff that words fail to accurately explain. We can't bring sight to our blind eyes. We can't transform our thought processes and change deeply ingrained bad habits. We can't bring life into dead places in our hearts. But, the Holy Spirit can . . . when we ask Him to, and then allow Him to.

King David understood this way back in the Old Testament. Look at his prayer in Psalm 51:10–12:

> Create in me a clean heart, O God, and renew a steadfast spirit within me. Do not cast me away from Your presence, and do not take Your Holy Spirit from me. Restore to me the joy of Your salvation, and uphold me by Your generous Spirit.

The Holy Spirit does such wonderful work. The Bible calls Him the Helper (John 14:16–17); our life (Rom. 8:2, 10–11); the Spirit of truth (John 14:17); the Spirit of adoption (Rom. 8:15–16); and the Spirit of holiness (Rom. 1:3–4). He is all those things for us.

When the pain of our orphan thinking becomes great enough that we are willing to do whatever it takes, the Holy Spirit does His work. When we give Him full permission (He won't force Himself on us) to do what He does—revealing truth, convicting of sin, comforting pain—things actually start to change. Bit by bit that orphan heart we've lived with for years is replaced by a new one: the heart of a daughter.

A DAUGHTER'S PRAYER

Oh Heavenly Father,

Thank You for calling me Your daughter—for loving me warts and all. Thank You for being a safe place for me and for giving me an eternal home.

I need to ask You to forgive me for all the years I've lived as an orphan even though You told me time and time again I was Your child. Please forgive me for having such a jealous and bitter heart, despising others for the blessings You were giving them. I was afraid nothing good was ever going to come to me. I see now that this is a lie, and I'm so sorry for believing it.

Please forgive me for all the years I worked to get the approval of people when all along You were longing to pour upon me more approval than I could have comprehended. I now accept my place at Your table as Your daughter, and I know Your plans for me are good. I know Your inheritance for me is good. I choose to believe the truth of Your Word about my life and the importance of it. I take my rightful position as a joint heir with Christ!

I love You,

Your daughter—the daughter of the King

WHAT ABOUT YOU?
OWNING UP TO ORPHAN WAYS

1. Take a look at the chart in appendix A. List three orphan heart tendencies you see in your own life: (For example: source of comfort — seek comfort in counterfeit affections)

   a. _____

   b. _____

   c. _____

2. Write what the chart says would be found in the heart of God's child for the categories you listed above: (For example: source of comfort — seek quiet times with God)

   a. _____

   b. _____

   c. _____

3. Do the orphan tendencies you mentioned in number one seem to have an effect on the relationships in your life? If so, in what way?_____

   _____

   _____

   _____

   _____

   _____

   _____

4. How do you think your daily life would change if you started really living like a daughter of the King?_____

_____

_____

_____

_____

5. What would it be like to truly love others with no strings attached, with no fear, and with the ability to truly rejoice when they are blessed? _____

_____

_____

_____

6. What might try to keep you from letting the Mighty Counselor bring to light everything He needs to in order to replace your orphan heart with a heart of a daughter?

_____

_____

_____

_____

_____

PEP TALK: TAKE YOUR PLACE

Most of us have never considered ourselves orphans. I know I never did—that is, until I saw all the orphan heart tendencies that were alive and well in my life. When I first saw all of this going on in me, I felt a bit disappointed in myself. But calling out the orphan heart in us isn't something to feel guilty about. It's really something to be excited about because there's a 100 percent effective remedy: taking our rightful place as children of God.

It's so important to remember that this "heart transplant" isn't accomplished by our own effort. We don't have to add anything to our religious "to do" list. We simply need to allow the Holy Spirit to reveal the truth about our identity as a daughter—to show us all that has been given to us and all that we have a right to. It really is like finding out a distant relative has left a huge inheritance for you in a safety deposit box. You've got the choice to receive the inheritance or not. Why would you want to deny it?

FORWARD FOCUS: CHILDREN OF GOD

- John 1:12—But as many as received Him, to them He gave the right to become **children of God**, to those who believe in His name.

- Romans 8:16 — The Spirit Himself bears witness with our spirit that we are **children of God**.
- Philippians 2:15 — That you may become blameless and harmless, **children of God** without fault in the midst of a crooked and perverse generation, among whom you shine as lights in the world.
- 1 John 3:1 — Behold what manner of love the Father has bestowed on us, that we should be called **children of God**! Therefore the world does not know us, because it did not know Him.
- 1 John 3:2 — Beloved, now we are **children of God**; and it has not yet been revealed what we shall be, but we know that when He is revealed, we shall be like Him, for we shall see Him as He is.
- 1 John 5:2 — By this we know that we love the **children of God**, when we love God and keep His commandments.

SEVEN

DIGGING DEEPER

Pull dandelions until the sun goes down,
But unless you destroy the roots,
You will awaken once again to a garden of weeds.

• • •

You may have heard this before, but I can't think of a better analogy to describe what happened in my life the day Father God took me even deeper—painfully deeper into my own heart (a journey I could not have taken as an orphan). Here's the question: What should you get when you throw a very small pebble into a quiet pond? Very small ripples, of course. Well, one day that small pebble caused a tidal wave of emotion in my life.

THE PEBBLE

The day was beautiful. It was sunny and warm—a perfect Saturday. The occasion: a baby shower. Around fifty women from my church had gathered to lavish a young expectant mother with gifts and to share words of blessing and advice.

105

The food was great. The fellowship, sweet. All was going well until the pebble dropped.

The mother of the expectant mother called for a time of prayer. This is something the women of my church almost always do: pray for the delivery, the baby, and the new family life to come. Since the group was so large, the mother of the mother-to-be handpicked a few women to come forward. One by one she invited each elder's wife in attendance. She invited them all . . . but me.

THE TIDAL WAVE

This dropped pebble didn't cause a ripple in me. It was more like a tidal wave. I couldn't believe what was happening. Neither could Sabby.

SABBY: How can she leave you out?

FAT CHRISTIAN WOMAN: I don't know. I am an elder's wife too!

SABBY: Oh, my gosh, I feel so bad for you. Why would she do that to you?

FAT CHRISTIAN WOMAN: I don't know. What is wrong with me?

SABBY: I don't really want to get into all that's wrong with you right now, but it's obvious that she doesn't like you very much. I guess your prayers aren't wanted.

Feelings of rejection rose in me faster than . . . well, pretty darn fast. I felt like I was going to throw up. A cold chill ran up and down my spine while hot tears sprang to my eyes. I thought I was going to have a meltdown.

Luckily for me every head was bowed and every eye was closed. The praying had begun. I sank as far back into a corner as I could and took several deep breaths as I tried to keep myself from yelping like a wounded cat. Tears kept trying to claw their way out of my eyes, as I dove deep within the recesses of my mind for some sort of rescue—perhaps a thought that would distract me, helping me to make it through these prayers with some composure. I needed something really good. Something funny would do the trick.

THE DEAD COW AND THE DOG

The thought I landed on was kind of funny, I guess. But it was mostly just plain gross.

I realize this may seem disturbing, but what I chose to meditate on while a sweet and holy moment was occurring on the other side of the room was . . . my dog sniffing a dead cow's backside. Now, before you judge me, I didn't *create* this thought. The scene actually happened earlier that very morning right outside my kitchen window. Living on a farm, visions such as this are quite common. I couldn't help it that this particular memory happened to come into my mind at just that (perfect) time.

As soon as the last amen was said, I put on the best fake smile I could and hugged anyone who happened to be standing in the way along my path to the door. I told the last woman I saw that I was so sorry I had to leave early, but that I had somewhere else to be. I nearly sprinted to my van, started it up, and peeled out of the gravel driveway—tires spitting rocks at the family dog. Tears finally broke through the barricade I had put up and rushed down my face in rivers. I drove away from those women I had known for years—mentally shooting them the bird. (I know . . . I was bad.)

A MOUTHFUL FOR GOD

Home at last, I threw open my front door—startling my sweet husband who gave me the "What on earth happened to you?" look—and ran as quickly as I could to my bedroom. I threw my purse on the floor, and I threw myself on the bed. Face down. Legs and arms sprawled out. And I cried. And I cried. And then I cried some more.

Then I let God have it.

FAT CHRISTIAN WOMAN: What is wrong with me? Why don't people like me? Why do I get hurt everywhere I go? Why did you make me this way? Why? Why?

When He could slip in a few words of His own, He answered.

FATHER GOD: Do you really want to know?

FAT CHRISTIAN WOMAN: Of course I want to know.
I can't live like this anymore! I hate the way I feel.

FATHER GOD: Okay, then. Get quiet a minute and
take My hand. I'm going to show you something.

FAT CHRISTIAN WOMAN: Okay. What is it?

MEMORY FROM HELL

Into my mind came a childhood memory. I was seven or eight years old at the time. I was visiting my aunt in Florida, and even though I didn't want to stay without my mom, she left me there to play with my cousins. Not long after mom left, my aunt left for work, and we kids were entrusted to the care of my uncle.

"Time to play a game, kiddos," Uncle said. "You know the one." Oh, I knew the one, all right. I'd played it before—a type of hide-and-seek. Only we didn't hide. Our underwear did. Uncle watched as we slid off our panties, and then he'd go hide them. If we found them, we won and got to pick the next activity. If we lost—well, he got to pick. And he always won.

He won that day, too, and the next thing I knew my little naked body was pushed to the floor, hands bound, rag shoved in my mouth, and innocence taken as tears streaked my little girl cheeks.

FAT CHRISTIAN WOMAN: Oh, God, not this memory again.

FATHER GOD: Yes. Keep watching.

FAT CHRISTIAN WOMAN: But how could You let that happen to me? Wasn't I cute enough? Wasn't I sweet enough? Didn't my life matter at all?

FATHER GOD: Keep watching.

At that time a new character entered my memory—one I never remembered seeing there before. He was ugly. He was dark. He walked up to my little body, knelt down on the floor so he could speak right into my ear, and he said, "You are trash, little girl. No one loves you. Your life isn't even worth protecting. Even your mom left you here." Then he looked right into my eyes, smiled a grin that was pure evil, stood, and walked away.

Back on my bed more tears came.

A LINGERING LIE

FAT CHRISTIAN WOMAN: That was the devil, wasn't it? The devil was there?

FATHER GOD: That's right, sweet girl. He spoke lies right into your very soul that day—lies you've believed ever since.

FAT CHRISTIAN WOMAN: I have? As a little girl,

when I felt so much rejection, I was just believing the lie?

FATHER GOD: Yes.

FAT CHRISTIAN WOMAN: As a teenager, when I was desperate for boys to like me, no matter what it took, I was believing the lie?

FATHER GOD: Yes.

FAT CHRISTIAN WOMAN: Every Sunday that I left church hurt because I wasn't included in this meeting or that—I was believing the lie?

FATHER GOD: Yes. You believed the lies. Now, let me show you one more thing.

THE HONEST TRUTH

Back in that room where my little girl body lay, another new figure appeared in the scene. He sat in the corner of the room on the floor with His arms wrapped tightly around His knees. He was rocking back and forth in agony, tears streaming down His face as He looked straight into my eyes.

FAT CHRISTIAN WOMAN: It's Jesus, isn't it?

FATHER GOD: Yes. It is My Son.

FAT CHRISTIAN WOMAN: He was there?

FATHER GOD: Yes, He was.

FAT CHRISTIAN WOMAN: Why didn't He get up and protect me? How could He just sit there like that?

FATHER GOD: He didn't just sit there. He got up—up on the Cross to protect you. He saved the deepest part of you—the part that will never die. He protected the part of you that responds to My voice. His heart bled for you—My heart bleeds for you. You are My beloved. Your life matters to Me.

FAT CHRISTIAN WOMAN: I see . . . but I still don't understand why He didn't stop my uncle from doing what he did. I thought Jesus could do anything He wanted.

FATHER GOD: Anything but take back the gift I gave at the beginning of time—free will. When I created human beings, I chose to give them freedom rather than make them robots despite the high cost to my heart. Your uncle perverted his free will.

NO MORE TIDAL WAVES

Words fall very short of describing the kind of pain I was feeling after that encounter with God, but under the ache a very broken part of my heart was being mended. Seeing that vision of pure evil whispering into my little soul made me furious. And the fact that the enemy chose a moment when I was the most vulnerable—the most afraid—to tell me such a crippling lie made me physically ill.

After years of living as an emotional basket case, truth was finding its way into the cracks in my heart. After years of being robbed of true friendship, healthy relationships, and peaceful living, I would take no more. No more feeling rejected at every turn. No more tidal waves.

When I look back now on that baby shower, I experience nothing but laughter. I can see that the only thing wrong that day was my deeply wounded heart. I know I was not intentionally left out. I know I was completely loved. What happened is the devil took advantage of a simple human oversight, knowing it would devastate me. He knew my weakness, and it's his job to attack every chance he gets. He does it to you too.

BUT I'M NOT WOUNDED

For many years — as a Christian — I did not think of myself as wounded. As a matter of fact, I was quite averse to talking about issues that seemed in any way related to psychobabble. Although I wouldn't balk at simply coming to terms with one's past, I believed that was where it needed to end. After all, once a gal becomes a Christian and is made new, what need is there to navel gaze? What could possibly be gained from dredging up (and possibly even creating) old memories? What a waste of time.

And in addition to my own thoughts on the matter, I didn't think God wanted to dredge up the past either. His Son died on the Cross for our sins and our wounds, once and for all. Why would we want to bring up anything from the past after such a sacrifice had been made on our behalf?

What a slap in the face it would be to Jesus if we should feel the need to revisit the days before we got saved. No way. Every good Christian knows that once you've come to Christ you are made new. No looking back. Enough said.

Wow.

Was I ever mistaken.

REALITY CHECK: WE'RE ALL WOUNDED

Try as we will to deny it, the truth is we're all wounded. No matter how much we attempt to convince ourselves that our very personal sinner's prayer did the trick, life has a way of proving otherwise. If the decision to follow Jesus in and of itself has the power to change so much in us, why is there still sin abounding in the church? Why do at least four out of ten *pastors* admit to viewing pornography on the Internet?[9] Because pain seeks pleasure, that's why—and a lot of Christians are in perpetual pain.

Well, what about the part of the Bible that says we are new creatures in Christ once we are born again (2 Cor. 5:17)? Well, it is true. When we accept Jesus into our lives we assume a new position or status before God; the Holy Spirit comes to live in our spirit and a divine new beginning occurs (John 14:23; 1 Cor. 6:19). That is truth.

But, what about the other parts of us? Our body and soul? Are those made perfectly new at the altar? Someone would have to be in seriously deep denial to say yes to that. I don't think we have to look much further than the mirror to see the truth of this matter. Gray hair? Wrinkles? No . . . not perfected.

And what about our soul—the area of our mind, will, and emotions? Is it perfected all at once? Just look at what you are experiencing in your life to answer that question. Depression, anger, jealousy, fear, anxiety, self-pity? If you feel any of these—ever—your soul is not perfected. And if we're not perfect, we're imperfect, and another word for that is *wounded*.

WHAT IS AN EMOTIONAL WOUND?

In order to understand what an emotional wound is, we've got to recognize one important point. We all have emotional needs, just as we have physical needs.

If I go without getting one of my physical needs met for long enough, I become physically sick. And going without some physical needs long enough, such as water or food, leads to death. The same can be said of our emotional needs. When we go without getting one of them met, we become emotionally sick. A painful void is created, and we'll do nearly anything it takes to fill it.

FOUR EMOTIONAL NEEDS

It is common knowledge that human beings have emotional needs. Depending on where you look, the list of these needs can be quite detailed and lengthy. Even though mental health professionals may state these needs in slightly different ways, the following list is an accurate summary of the four basic emotional needs of mankind.

1. **Unconditional love.** This refers to love that is expressed (spoken) to us in appropriate verbal and physical ways such as words, hugs, and kisses.
2. **Security.** This means a *feeling* of total security, a physical and emotional safety which is more than just having a roof over our heads.
3. **Praise.** This means being verbally affirmed, valued, and admired by another.
4. **Purpose.** This is a reason for us personally to be alive and to have a feeling of hope for the future.

Now, in God's perfect plan, our parents were meant to take care of these needs for us as a model of what God Himself intended to do throughout our lives. But, as Dr. Sandra Wilson says, "Even the most well-meaning parents unintentionally inflict hurts by being unprepared, unavailable, or, more likely a combination of both."[10] A wound is created no matter the motivation of the "wounder." It doesn't have to be a direct assault such as in sexual abuse. In fact, some of the worst wounds are caused when a fulfillment of a need has been *omitted* rather than an abuse *committed*. And wounds don't have to be the result of our parents' actions. Even in our adult years, we continue to suffer wounding at the hands of people in our lives—sometimes people we've put our trust into.

COUNTERFEITS

Because there are no perfect parents (or people in general, for that matter), there isn't one of us who has had all of our emotional needs met completely. And even if we had a wonderful childhood, there are times throughout our lives when our emotional needs don't feel met. So, think of this: If you were denied water for several days, what would be the first thing on your mind? *Getting water.* You would be tempted to drink anything resembling water—even a counterfeit—to get that need met, right? People will even drink their own urine in times of extreme thirst.

Now, what if we talk about an emotional need such as the need for praise? Say when you were a little girl no one ever told you how beautiful you were or how important your existence was. Or, now that you're grown, maybe it's been a really long time since you heard someone affirm you. What do you think becomes essential? That's right, *getting praise*. Now, even though you might be totally unaware of the reason, you might become compelled to get approval from anyone who will give it to you. A great analogy describes it this way: it's like walking around with an IV needle inserted in your arm and holding on to the other end, ready to stick it into anyone who comes your way so you can suck what you need out of them.

And what if your need for love seems unmet? That won't just go away. You'll still have a need for physical affection, and you may just settle for lust (maybe your own lust, or someone else's toward you) rather than real love.

Or if your need for security doesn't seem fully met, maybe now you'll feel driven to have the biggest and best of everything. Money has become your source of security and your need for it seems to grow and grow.

And what about purpose? If you don't feel you have a purpose, you might work yourself to death trying to make it to the top of the corporate ladder. Or you might offer to serve everywhere there's an opening at church so your pastor will pat you on the back and say, "What would we do without you around here?" Or maybe, in order to feel *really* important, you might have to start a ministry—any ministry.

The truth is, if we are doing any of these things in order to get our emotional needs met, we are going to counterfeit sources. The only real way to get needs met is from God Himself.

UNGODLY MOTIVATION

We can't be truly effective disciples of Jesus Christ when we are being led by a wounded heart because our motives will be twisted. Before we discuss what this means, let me say that I don't mean that *all* we do for the Lord in our wounded state is worthless. Absolutely not. In His goodness, our heavenly Father works all things for good in the lives of those who are called by Him for His purposes (Rom. 8:28). He uses our lives in spite of ourselves.

What's important to see, however, is that our motivation for service won't be totally pure if we are driven to serve *because* of our wounded heart, and that's sure to have a negative effect on whatever we are doing, be it serving, parenting, or whatever. Whether we are aware of it consciously or not, we will be seeking to meet our unmet emotional needs in almost everything we do. Our motives will be selfish rather than selfless like those of our Lord. His heart was whole. He wasn't emotionally wounded. To follow Him means to walk with Him closely, to know Him, and to know how to become more like Him. To be whole.

I remember that ever since I became a believer, I had a passion to serve the Lord. I wanted to do anything He would ask me to do, no matter what the cost. But it wasn't until I began to see my woundedness, and to receive healing for those wounds, that I have been able to truly serve *Him* rather than myself. This is a process, and I don't expect to be completely healed until heaven, but it is getting better all the time. I'm finally able to experience what it's like to love people with no strings attached.

GOD'S THOUGHTS ON THE MATTER

So what does God think about this issue of emotional wounds? Isn't it like telling Jesus His work on the Cross wasn't enough when we admit to still being wounded? No, it's not. In fact, God knows we are wounded and tells us so in the Bible:

- For I will restore health to you and heal you of your wounds. (Jeremiah 30:17)
- The LORD builds up Jerusalem; He gathers together the outcasts of Israel. He heals the brokenhearted and binds up their wounds. (Psalm 147:2–3)
- The Spirit of the LORD is upon Me, because He has anointed Me to preach the gospel to the poor; He has sent Me to heal the broken-hearted, to proclaim liberty to the captives and recovery of sight to the blind, to set at liberty those who are oppressed. (Luke 4:18)

These verses show that God is aware of our broken-heartedness, and it is His desire to heal us. And the wonderful thing is that He loves us enough to heal each and every one of our wounds individually—to take us to the places deep within us that need a divine touch by Him. He doesn't expect us to just get over anything. He cares enough to heal every wound inflicted upon my heart since the time of my birth.

He loves me enough to take me there—to escort me to the entry point of each and every lie I've believed so that He can displace the lies with truth. He wants to do that for you too.

FOUR STEPS TOWARD HEALING

There is nothing we can do to get rid of our emotional wounds except to get them healed. We cannot yell them away (rebuke them), nor do we need to ask God to forgive us for having emotional wounds. That would be as ridiculous as pointing a finger at a deep, bloody puncture in our thigh and shouting, "I rebuke you in the name of Jesus. Be gone with you!" And just slapping a bandage over the top of it isn't going to do anything either. What that bleeding sore needs isn't to be scolded or hidden, it needs to be healed. So does our heart.

So how does that healing happen? Well, the short answer is, supernaturally. It is a divine work of God that cannot be put into a one-size-fits-all formula. It truly is an *experience* and not a procedure. However, there is a basic description of what transpires when we are being healed. First, we admit we are wounded. (If you're still not sure you're wounded, check out the list of personality types associated with emotional wounds in appendix B.) Second, we entrust our hearts to Father God (which can only happen when we truly *know* Him and believe we are His child). Third, we allow the Holy Spirit to bring to mind times in our lives when we were hurt and to then reveal to us the lies we started believing. Fourth, we allow Him to tell us the truth of the matter. When we choose to believe it, the power of God's truth overpowers the influence of the lie, and healing starts to take place. It really does.

In his book *Telling Yourself the Truth*, Dr. William Backus calls this process the "steps to becoming the happy person you were meant to be." He says we must locate our misbeliefs, remove them, and replace them with truth.[11] I believe this is exactly what God means when He tells us to renew our minds (Eph. 4:23). The neat thing is *He* actually does the renewing. All we have to do is submit to the process by jumping up on the operating table and letting Him have His way.

Easier said than done, right? Some of us have been very deeply wounded, and trusting anyone — God included — with those places takes real guts. But you will never experience all the victory, power, and love that God has already deposited in your spirit if you don't give Him an all-access pass to your soul. We've got to allow Him to take us into His arms and pour the healing ointment of His love and truth right into every single crevice of our brokenness. Then we will be like King David when he prayed:

> Search me, O God, and know my [wounded] heart; try me, and know my anxieties; and see if there is any wicked way in me, and lead me in the way everlasting. (Psalm 139:23–24)

GETTING THE REAL STUFF

As healing occurs in our hearts, we will get more and more of our emotional needs met from the right source—God. After all, He's the one who created our emotions. Isn't He the most logical one to go to for their ongoing care?

Let's take a look at some proof from the Bible that our Father is taking care of us. The next time you doubt your worth, purpose, or God's love for you, consult His words to you:

Unconditional love
- Jeremiah 31:3—My Father's love for me is everlasting. I have always been loved by Him.
- John 3:16—My Father gave His only Son to die so I could know how much He loves me.
- John 16:26–27—My Father loves me so much, He wants a personal relationship with me.
- Ephesians 3:19—My Father wants me to be so full of His love that I'm overflowing.

Security
- Romans 8:38–39—Nothing (not even my faults) can separate me from God's love.
- Colossians 3:3—I am securely hidden in Christ in the Father.
- 2 Timothy 1:7—I am filled with power, love, and a sound mind.
- 1 John 5:18—The devil has no right to touch me.

- Isaiah 66:12–13 — My Father wants to comfort and hold me tenderly.

Affirmation

- Psalm 149:4 — My Father tells me that He takes pleasure in me.
- Jeremiah 29:11 — My Father's thoughts toward me are always good and filled with hope for me.
- Song of Solomon 1:15–16 — My Father tells me in poetry that I am beautiful and pleasant in His eyes.
- John 14:23 — My Father approves of me so much that He made His home within me.

Purpose

- Matthew 5:13–14 — I am the salt and light of the earth.
- Acts 1:8 — I am a witness of God's goodness to the world.
- 2 Corinthians 5:18 — I am a minister of reconciliation for God.
- Philippians 4:13 — I am a powerhouse in Christ.

Our heavenly Father definitely has all our needs covered. If we can see the truth of His heart in His Word, and receive

His love into our hearts, it becomes easier and easier to trust Him. We can also trust that He will send *tangible expressions* of His love when we need it. We will get the healthy hugs we need. We will get an encouraging word. We will have the material items we need. But we won't be *desperate* for them. Any praise from man or any earthly achievement becomes the cherry on top—not the whole sundae.

A PLEA FOR CONTINUED HEALING

Oh, Abba Daddy,

I love You and thank You for Your amazing love for me. I choose today to receive Your love instead of resisting it, and I choose to trust my whole heart to You.

I ask You to continue to show me the dark places in my heart— places that have not yet seen the light of Your truth. I don't want to live my life believing lies anymore. I don't want to keep falling into the trap of ungodly thoughts and behaviors. I want to live the abundant life You've promised me. I need Your help to become whole, Father.

I hand over my complete heart to You. I lay down any pride that would keep me from being truly transparent before You.

And I ask You, Father, to forgive me for all the years my service for You was motivated by unmet emotional needs. I am so sorry. Please be quick to convict me each and every time my motivation slips off track again. I want to be like Jesus—loving others because all His needs were met in You.

And I ask You to forgive me, also, for going to counterfeits to get my need met instead of You. All You've ever wanted to do is provide for my heart. I am sorry I didn't believe that before, but I do now. Please help me to see more and more how much You love me. Change me completely, Father. I am Yours.

Amen

WHAT ABOUT YOU?
WEIGHTY WOUNDS

1. Take a look at appendix B in the back of the book. Which of these personalities do you find most difficult to deal with in your life? _____

2. Do you think your personality resembles any of those on the list? If so, which one(s)? _____

   _____

3. Are you hesitant to admit that you are emotionally wounded? _____

4. Do you think it's possible for any human being to have his or her emotional needs met perfectly at all times (apart from getting them met by God)? Explain. _____

   _____

   _____

   _____

5. Look at the scale below. Where do you think your beliefs fall with regard to how God views your emotional wounds:

"Just get over it already. You're saved."   "Please let Me heal each of your wounds."

0   1   2   3   4   5

6. Jesus often asked people a question like this: "Do you want to be healed?" He didn't ask to get permission, He asked because being healed often requires a lot from people emotionally. It requires being willing to let go of our claim on our wounds—any identity we've been getting from our hurts. With that in mind, if Jesus were to ask you the question, what would you say? _____

_____

_____

_____

PEP TALK: IT HURTS SO GOOD

There's no denying it. There's nothing fun about looking at a wound. And the deeper the injury, the harder to behold. But there's nothing sweeter than the feeling of healing that comes after that encounter. It's kind of like childbirth.

There's nothing quite so painful as the experience of labor and delivery, but the beauty of the child nearly erases all the pain. That's why women all over the world continue to bear children—even multiple times. The pain is worth it.

Just as with childbirth, we all have different support needs when it comes to our journey to healing. Some of us will "go natural," needing only quiet time with the Holy Spirit who will bring to light all we need to see. Others of us will take all the support we can get ("I know I just got here, but give me the epidural"). Either way, it's glorious to the Father. It's the end result He's looking forward to, and if we seek Him, He will be there every step of the way.

FORWARD FOCUS: HEALING

- Psalm 41:4—I said, "LORD, be merciful to me; **heal** my soul, for I have sinned against You."
- Isaiah 61:1—The Spirit of the Lord GOD is upon Me, because the LORD has anointed Me to preach good tidings to the poor; He has sent Me to **heal** the brokenhearted, to proclaim liberty to the captives, and the opening of the prison to those who are bound.
- Isaiah 58:8—Then your light shall break forth like the morning, your **healing** shall spring forth speedily, and your righteousness shall go before you; the glory of the LORD shall be your rear guard.

- Jeremiah 33:6 — Behold, I will bring it health and **healing**; I will heal them and reveal to them the abundance of peace and truth.
- Malachi 4:2 — But to you who fear My name the Sun of Righteousness shall arise with **healing** in His wings.
- Matthew 4:23 — And Jesus went about all Galilee, teaching in their synagogues, preaching the gospel of the kingdom, and **healing** all kinds of sickness and all kinds of disease among the people.
- Luke 9:6 — So they departed and went through the towns, preaching the gospel and **healing** everywhere.
- Luke 9:11 — But when the multitudes knew it, they followed Him; and He received them and spoke to them about the kingdom of God, and **healed** those who had need of healing.
- Act 10:38 — How God anointed Jesus of Nazareth with the Holy Spirit and with power, who went about doing good and **healing** all who were oppressed by the devil, for God was with Him.

EIGHT

FORGIVING AND FESSING UP

● ● ●

Forgiveness. It's just one of those words that doesn't always evoke warm fuzzies—unless, of course, we're talking about the forgiveness extended to *ourselves*. It's kind of like the word *mortgage*. While we all want to qualify for a loan so we can get our cute little house, we also know that we're gonna be writing a big fat check every month. Likewise, we all want to qualify for forgiveness, but on the other hand, it's quite costly. You see, when we receive forgiveness, we must also be willing to give it.

Whether we like the thought of forgiving people or not, it is something God absolutely requires. He requires forgiveness because it represents a total trust in Him. A trust that He will take complete and total care of the wrongs that have been done to us—including dealing with those who have hurt us. And trusting someone with all of that isn't always easy.

NO DENYING IT

It's important to take a look at what God has to say about forgiveness—just in case we're tempted to minimize its role in our lives.

> Then Peter came to Him and said, "Lord, how often shall my brother sin against me, and I forgive him? Up to seven times?" Jesus said to him, "I do not say to you, up to seven times, but up to seventy times seven." (Matthew 18:21–22)

Seventy times seven was Jesus' way of saying "forgive forever." And notice that Jesus doesn't put any disclaimers on it such as "unless someone has made a fool of you," or "unless someone steals something extremely precious." No. It's just "you must forgive, and you must forgive forever."

And how about this one:

> And do not grieve the Holy Spirit of God, by whom you were sealed for the day of redemption. Let all bitterness, wrath, anger, clamor, and evil speaking be put away from you, with all malice. And be kind to one another, tenderhearted, forgiving one another, even as God in Christ forgave you. (Ephesians 4:30–32)

We see here that God isn't asking us to do anything He

hasn't done first. He's forgiven us, which gives Him the credibility to ask us to do the same. With kindness and love, He asks us to travel a road with which He's personally familiar. He knows the way is good.

We also see in those verses that our bitterness, anger, and ill will toward one another actually *grieve* the Holy Spirit. It distresses Him. It makes Him heavy hearted and sorrowful. Our lack of forgiveness thus works against us. We definitely don't want to hurt the heart of the very One whose help we need the most. No, we need as much of God as we can get since hope and healing come from Him.

WHAT IF I DON'T FORGIVE?

So, right now you might be thinking, "Okay, I get that I'm being asked to forgive, but what happens if I don't?" It's a good question, kind of like asking, "What happens if I don't pay my mortgage?" And the honest answer is, you will be able to enjoy your cute little house just long enough to decorate the rooms, but if you refuse to pay long enough, legal action will be taken against you.

It's the same with forgiveness. Once we've accepted the forgiveness God extends to us, He allows us to enjoy it—to thrill at the thought that we've been given such an amazing gift. And then He asks us to pay. No, He doesn't ask us to pay for *our own* forgiveness. It really is a free gift. But He asks us to forgive in return. It is costly, but if we choose not to do it, we will pay a much greater price.

FREEBIRD AND THE KING

There's a great example of this in the Bible. It's from Matthew 18.

In the story there was a king who had some servants who owed him lots of money (let's say tens of thousands of dollars). He was putting them all in jail for the debt, when one of the servants had the nerve to appeal to the mercy of the king. He begged, "Please don't do this. I will repay you." He must have been really convincing, because the king not only lets him out of going to jail, but forgives the entire debt and sends him on his merry way.

Now, this forgiven servant (we'll call him Freebird for short) enjoys his freedom for a while and then decides he's gonna call in some debts that are owed to him. Freebird has this person who owes him something like a hundred bucks, and he demands to be paid immediately. Of course, the guy begs for time to pay (just as Freebird himself did from the king), but he is denied it. Freebird sends this guy to debtor's prison. No mercy.

Now, what do you think happens when the king hears about this? Well, he is furious. In fact, this is what he says to Freebird: "You wicked servant! I forgave you all that debt because you begged me. Should you not also have had compassion on your fellow servant, just as I had pity on you?" (verses 32–33). The king was so angry that the Bible says he delivered Freebird not to jail, but to the *torturers* until he would pay back his original debt in full. (Can you say clipped wings?)

Here's the real kicker. Right after Jesus gets done telling Peter this whole story, He says this in verse 35: "So my heavenly Father also will do to you if each of you, from his heart, does not forgive his brother his trespasses." Ouch!

ISN'T THAT KIND OF HARSH?

If you're like me, you read those words spoken by Jesus and wonder, "Does God really deliver us to *torturers* just because we won't forgive? I mean, come on. That doesn't seem fair." I agree, it does seem tough . . . at first. But, let's take a closer look.

I think it's safe for me to assume that we're all okay with the beginning of the story, right? We'd all agree that we—like Freebird—have been forgiven much. I know I have. I was (and still am) in desperate need of mercy.

And I think we'd all agree that Freebird was being a huge jerk when he refused to forgive the guy who owed him so very little. What a creep, huh? (We would *never* do that . . . would we?) In fact, I think we probably all feel a little sense of justice when Freebird gets delivered to the torturers. After all, doesn't he deserve it? (Hey, pass me one of those sharp pokers.)

But then God turns the spotlight onto us, and this is where we stop liking the story. He compares us directly to

Freebird—like we're being as big a jerk as he was when we don't forgive—and this is where confusion can set in if we don't remember the heart of our Father.

At this point we've got to pan out for a broader view. We've got to think of the full nature of God, and not just focus on a close-up of Jesus saying (in a cynical tone, of course) "You're going to the torturers!" (followed by evil chuckle). This is not what's going on here.

We've got to think this one through. First, remember, we believe that God is good, don't we? I hope you answered yes. And if God is good (in fact the epistle writer defines God as love in 1 John 4:8), would He ever ask us to do something that isn't good for us? Of course not.

When He asks us to forgive, He's got our best interest in mind. In fact, *not forgiving* is very harmful to us.

Think of it this way: If your child, or a child you love, was doing something that was bad for her—in fact could hurt her for the rest of her life—wouldn't you do anything to stop it? What if the only thing that would work was allowing circumstances to get a bit uncomfortable for her for a while? Maybe even painful? Would you do it? It takes an amazing amount of love for someone to make a decision like that because most often, allowing uncomfortable circumstances in a child's life means accepting them for ourselves too. (Nothing fun about watching a grounded child mope around the house.)

God loves us enough to let circumstances become as uncomfortable as it takes. He will even allow us to be delivered to torturers if that's how stubborn we insist on being. And though He does not want us to be there, because of His great love for us He will allow us to sit in debtor's jail a while.

THE TORTURERS

When you close your eyes and imagine the torturers, what do you see? I picture the monstrous evil characters from Middle Earth in *The Lord of the Rings*. I see massive bodies covered with calcified warts topped off with one-eyed heads that ooze pus and sweat. But that's not really what they are.

The torturers aren't that frightening, or else we would spend as little time with them as we possibly could. No, the torturers we deal with are far more subtle. In fact, it can take years to recognize them.

ENTITLEMENT

Let me tell you about some of my former torturers, so you can get an idea of how they work. The first one was Entitlement. I suffered under the hands of this taskmaster for many years, for it is so convincing in its approach. What Entitlement tells us is so easy to believe because it appeals to our selfish nature—any of our orphan thinking that might be hanging around. Here's what Entitlement told me:

> **ENTITLEMENT:** You have a total right to be bitter . . . and angry.
> **FAT CHRISTIAN WOMAN:** I do, don't I?

ENTITLEMENT: You're darn straight. No one should say things like that about you. Until she apologizes to you properly, she doesn't deserve anything from you.

FAT CHRISTIAN WOMAN: That's right! No one's going to treat me that way.

See, it looks so fair—so right—on the surface. But really, it's a trap. A trap to stay stuck in pride and selfish living. To stay stuck in an "all-about-me" mindset rather than an "all-about-Him" life of freedom.

SELF-PITY

Here's another of my torturers: Self-pity. Self-pity and Entitlement often work together as a team.

SELF-PITY: You've really had to endure a lot of hardship in your life, haven't you?

FAT CHRISTIAN WOMAN: Yes, I really have. (*Deep sigh.*)

SELF-PITY: No one really understands your pain, do they?

FAT CHRISTIAN WOMAN: Not really. How did you know?

SELF-PITY: Oh, I just know. No one really cares either, do they? They're all content to go on with their happy lives and let you writhe in your pain.

FAT CHRISTIAN WOMAN: I know. If people only knew how many tears I cry each day. Nobody likes me.

VICTIM MENTALITY

Maybe you'll recognize my next torturer: Victim Mentality.

VICTIM MENTALITY: I can't believe you're able to get out of bed in the mornings. After all, you have been abused at every turn.

FAT CHRISTIAN WOMAN: I know. But shouldn't I be doing more in my life?

VICTIM MENTALITY: No! How can you expect any more out of yourself? My gosh! Most people don't ever experience that kind of abuse. You're doing just fine. Just fine.

FAT CHRISTIAN WOMAN: But doesn't the Bible tell me I can do great things because of Jesus?

VICTIM MENTALITY: It does, but you were abused! You're a graduate from the school of very, very hard knocks. You can't forget that.

BITTERNESS

Or how about my next torturer: Bitterness?

BITTERNESS: I just can't imagine that there is a fire hot enough for all of those people to burn in.

FAT CHRISTIAN WOMAN: I totally agree.

BITTERNESS: Truth be told, I think they should have to pay for each and every thing they've done to you. Chinese water torture perhaps?

FAT CHRISTIAN WOMAN: Yeah, and sleep deprivation. That will show them. They will pay.

UNFORGIVENESS IS STRESS

Living with these torturers is not really living. Though they can seem to be on our side, these mental strongholds truly subject us to a slow death—keeping us from joy, peace, and the experience of giving and receiving real love. The torturers keep us securely locked in unforgiveness.

In their book, *The Quick-Reference Guide to Biblical Counseling*, Drs. Tim Clinton and Ron Hawkins say this about this prison: "Unforgiveness is a cancer that eats away at the very soul of a person."[12]

Not only does refusing to forgive others affect our emotional life, but there have been scientific studies conducted that connect unforgiveness with poor physical health. According to one report, "The core components of unforgiveness (e.g., anger, hostility, blame, fear) have been associated with health and disease outcomes."[13] In studies like this, unforgiveness is considered a stressor in our lives, and can be just as responsible for stress-related diseases as our Post-it-Note-covered refrigerators are.

JAIL BREAK: FORGIVENESS

Now most stressors in our life can be dealt with by adding a few hours of peaceful stretching into the schedule here and there. Not so with unforgiveness. This one requires a different commitment—a heart-level commitment. It requires a willingness to listen to what God is trying to tell us and to move toward trusting Him with all we can of our hearts. After taking a good look at the alternative, doesn't this seem the healthier choice?

It was easier for me to become willing to forgive when I learned a bit more about what forgiveness really means. For many years I falsely believed that by forgiving someone I was saying that what they did to me was okay and that I had to actually *like* the person afterward. But, that's not what forgiveness is. In fact, God himself is never okay with the wrongs done to us. He has some pretty harsh words for those who hurt His children:

> But whoever causes one of these little ones who
> believe in Me to stumble, it would be better for
> him if a millstone were hung around his neck, and
> he were thrown into the sea. (Mark 9:42)

Taking steps toward forgiveness is so much easier when we know what it does and does not mean.

FORGIVENESS DOES NOT MEAN:

- what was done to me is okay
- I have to forget—putting on a fake smile as if nothing was ever done wrong
- the person who hurt me gets away with what was done
- I have to trust the people who hurt me ever again (If you step on my foot every time you walk by I can forgive you, but I'm going to start moving my foot away.)
- I have to lie down and take more abuse

FORGIVENESS DOES MEAN:

- I will work through a hard process, but one well worth the pain
- I am set free (not vice versa) from the power my offender has had over me
- I trust God enough to take my offenders off of my hook and put them on God's hook
- torturers (mental strongholds) are destroyed
- a door is opened up for me to have a much deeper relationship with God

THE WORST OFFENDER FIRST

For me, forgiveness started with the worst offender first—the one whose abuse had caused years and years of pain in my life: my uncle. It might be a different journey for you, but

I'll tell you . . . for me, getting that one over with first made the rest seem like a downhill ride.

Let me say this . . . forgiving my uncle happened in stages, and they weren't all easy. Most importantly, I couldn't have done it without believing with all my heart that God would deal with the man. Even now, even after experiencing the freedom of forgiving him, the justice bone in me finds peace in knowing that one day my uncle will have to settle that account with God. But I won't have to be a part of that conversation. My part has been settled.

The most powerful part of forgiving my uncle was supernatural. The Holy Spirit had to do some pretty serious stretching of my thinking process to get me through it. He had to help me see some things through His eyes because mine were blinded by my pain.

The forgiveness that I eventually was able to grant from my *heart* (as Jesus asks us to) started its journey in my *head*. And just as it had happened so many times before, this session with the Mighty Counselor required a journey back in time — even before my time.

> **MIGHTY COUNSELOR:** Teasi, do you think you've fully forgiven your uncle?
> **FAT CHRISTIAN WOMAN:** I don't know. I guess so.
> **MIGHTY COUNSELOR:** Well, what do you feel when you think of him?

FAT CHRISTIAN WOMAN: I feel sort of sick to my stomach. My stomach gets tight.

MIGHTY COUNSELOR: It doesn't look to me like forgiveness has taken its full course yet.

FAT CHRISTIAN WOMAN: You're probably right.

MIGHTY COUNSELOR: Do you want it to? (*Always the gentleman.*)

FAT CHRISTIAN WOMAN: Yes, I do. I want to be completely free.

MIGHTY COUNSELOR: Okay, good. That's what I want for you too. Are you willing to consider something you've never considered before?

FAT CHRISTIAN WOMAN: Yes, anything.

MIGHTY COUNSELOR: Okay, I want you to picture a little boy around five years old, about the age of your boy. Can you see him? He's got cute cheeks.

FAT CHRISTIAN WOMAN: Yes, I see him.

MIGHTY COUNSELOR: See him playing with a little toy—his favorite. His smile fades as he looks up at the door to his room. His father is standing there. The little boy cowers against the side of his bed hoping to disappear into the folds of his quilt, but it doesn't work. Dad comes for him after locking the door, and for the next hour the little boy is abused— in every way you can imagine.

FAT CHRISTIAN WOMAN: That's horrible. I can't believe a dad would do that to his own child.

MIGHTY COUNSELOR: Just before his dad leaves the room, he looks into the boy's scared little eyes and says, "This is all your fault. If you weren't such a freak I wouldn't have to do this stuff to you. You make me sick." The boy is left with a scarred body and a scarred heart. The boy is left with a lie.

FAT CHRISTIAN WOMAN: My heart is broken for that boy. Oh, my gosh. That's horrible. (*Tears.*)

MIGHTY COUNSELOR: That boy grew up believing he was a freak, and he began to believe other lies, as well. He started to believe that the only way he would ever be loved, ever be touched, was if he got that love from children. Adults were far too scary.

FAT CHRISTIAN WOMAN: Oh, God, is that my uncle?

MIGHTY COUNSELOR: Not exactly, but it is a story much like his. Your uncle was a young boy who at one time was very wounded, and at another time believed a lie about himself, and that lie grew. That lie eventually hurt you. It's one of those lies that destroys generations of my precious people.

FAT CHRISTIAN WOMAN: I see.

MIGHTY COUNSELOR: I know it's a huge, huge thing to ask, but do you think you can let me deal justly with the pain that was inflicted upon you? Can you give that boy over to me? That is forgiveness. I know this is requiring a lot of trust from you.

FAT CHRISTIAN WOMAN: I trust you. I choose to give him to you. I can forgive.

TURNED OVER TO THE AUTHORITY

The Holy Spirit knew exactly how to help me turn my case over to the Father's court where He would litigate the matter. It's what He wants to do for all of us. Look at this: "He heals the brokenhearted and binds up their wounds" (Ps. 147:3).

What's important about this verse is that the phrase "binds up" has a multilayered definition in the Hebrew language. It can mean not only to compress or wrap firmly, but also to *govern over*. So it seems God is saying that He not only wants to heal our broken hearts, but He wants to govern over the case. As the ultimate authority, He wants to deal with every aspect of our wounds—the healing and dealing with those who have hurt us.

Jesus, undeniably the most unfairly wounded and abused person to ever live, understood this important part of His destiny:

> [Jesus] who, when He was reviled, did not revile
> in return; when He suffered, He did not threaten,
> but committed Himself to Him who judges righ-
> teously. (1 Peter 2:23)

Jesus did not take vengeance into His own hands, when He most certainly had the power to do so. He committed it all to the Father. And if He trusted the Father to govern over His wounds, we can do the same in His strength. Jesus Himself tells us so:

> Most assuredly, I say to you, he who believes in Me, the works that I do he will do also; and greater works than these he will do, because I go to My Father. (John 14:12)

The Father has made every provision for us to be able to forgive. He fully understands our pain and never belittles it, but He knows what we need to do in order to be free from its continued power over us. He loves us enough to bring about the highest justice on our behalf.

ELECTIVE SURGERY

Now, I know there is a lot more to the story of my uncle's life than what I was able to imagine. I know there is a lot of personal responsibility at play too. That young wounded boy grew up to be a man who knew right from wrong . . . and he chose wrong. I see that now. But I also know that wounded people wound people. And somehow God's overwhelming mercy became just contagious enough for me to catch. That mercy became my get-out-of-jail card. It wasn't a get-out-of-jail-*free* card. Not at all. As you know, it cost this little girl quite a lot. Giving forgiveness to someone who had hurt me so deeply was like undergoing elective surgery with no anesthesia. But it brought me new life.

GUILT BY ASSOCIATION

Then there are those we need to forgive who are guilty only by association. For me this would be my parents and my aunt (the wife of my abuser). For you it might be a teacher, a sibling, or a best friend—anyone you felt could have done something to rescue you from your pain, even if they didn't realize they could have.

While many of these people didn't purposely or directly wound us, and some may not even realize we've been wounded at all, they are *participants in the trauma*, and forgiving them is an often overlooked part of full healing. It's easy to feel unmerciful and even selfish when we admit to needing to forgive those who didn't intentionally hurt us. It's also common to be afraid of what might happen to those relationships if we open up to our true feelings. But it is essential that we take this step. If left hidden in the dark, that need to forgive can begin to grow the moldy roots of bitterness. We really must trust God with knowing that He will protect the relationships we love so much. It's about our freedom.

OUR OWN GUILT

Our next step requires us to take an even closer look at sin—only this time, our own. The people who hurt us are not the only guilty ones. Along the way, there have been people we've hurt too. Even though we are not responsible for the wounds that have been inflicted upon us, we are responsible for the way we've lived as a result of those hurts. Sometimes we've hurt others simply out of our own pain, but no matter the reason for our actions we truly need to be forgiven.

I'll start by sharing a little about some of my own sin and by saying that I am so thankful God has loved me enough to walk me through my journey in stages I could handle. There is no way I would have been ready to face it all before I felt completely loved, healed, adopted, and forgiven. In His gentleness and goodness God waited until I could handle it, and then He sat me in front of the mirror . . . a three-way mirror . . . with fluorescent lighting. You know the kind I'm talking about, don't you? (Thank you, department stores.)

JUDGE NOT

I'm going to start with a scripture to set the stage:

> Judge not, and you shall not be judged. Condemn
> not, and you shall not be condemned. Forgive,
> and you will be forgiven. Give, and it will be given
> to you: good measure, pressed down, shaken
> together, and running over will be put into your
> bosom. For with the same measure that you use, it
> will be measured back to you. (Luke 6:37–38)

What this section of Scripture is saying is that when we plant some bad apple seeds, we really shouldn't be surprised when some time later we get some bad apples (the law of sowing and reaping). It is a spiritual law that God established. And spiritual laws are just as sure as the physical laws we've all grown to depend on. (Thank you, gravity.) Now, in God's goodness, He can shorten the "bad apple" season if He wants (and He often does), but that does not take us off the hook for planting season. We've got to own up to it.

An honest assessment of my own emotional farmland revealed that many a defective seed had been planted there. For years I was judgmental and condemning, and I *liked* it. Thoughts such as these were common for me: "I cannot believe she did *that*. How rude." Or "I would *never* wear that in public. Does this woman own a mirror?" Or even worse, "At least I'm not *that* fat. I'm actually skinny compared to her."

GOD REPELLENT: PRIDE

Judgment like that starts with only one thing: pride. And I'll admit there was an awful lot of that in me. Pride is not something we can continue to put up with in our lives if we expect to live life to the fullest. In order to achieve anything close to our best life, we're gonna need as much of God as we can get, and God doesn't like pride. Listen to this: "God resists the proud, but gives grace to the humble" (James 4:6).

God can't be around our pride; it literally repels Him. It's not that He doesn't *want* to be around us. There's nothing

He wants more. It's just that He *can't*. You see, when we are walking in pride we are living with a distorted view of our identity—either thinking too much or too little of ourselves—and we're not accepting what God says about us. Our pride actually causes us to call God a liar, which He's not too fond of. It's like we're asking God if we can take a seat on His throne for a bit, or going to the other extreme and curling up into a worthless ball under His feet. Neither is our rightful and true place, where God wants us to live.

GET RICH QUICK: HUMILITY

Humility, on the other hand, is accepting our position as God's beloved children and happily enjoying all the benefits *and struggles* that accompany that calling. God wants us to live like this because that's when He can help us the most. Remember, He gives His grace to the humble. God's grace in action is a powerful force. One we want to stay plugged into.

Listen to this:

By humility and the fear of the LORD are riches
and honor and life. (Proverbs 22:4)

Riches, honor, and life. Sounds like what all humanity is crying out for, doesn't it? Those things come by way of our humility, by our willingness to be meek and teachable—by our surrender to the perfect ways of God.

And not only does humility usher in blessings, it's the best pick-me-up you can find:

> Humble yourself in the sight of the Lord, and He
> will lift you up. (James 4:10)

Having the Lord pick us up when we're feeling down is far better than even the strongest iced mocha latte Starbucks can offer.

ALL-PURPOSE CLEANSER: REPENTANCE

Taking an honest look at our own sin can be difficult. I know this firsthand. It really broke my heart when I started to acknowledge how much judgment lived in me and how critical I had been at times in my life. But here's the sweet news. God's goodness draws us to repentance (Rom. 2:4). And when we confess our sins, God is ready to forgive us and clean us up (1 John 1:9). He says He will cleanse our unrighteousness.

God doesn't clean us so He can love us more. No way. He cleans us so we *feel clean*. We were actually forgiven once and for all when Jesus died on the Cross. But the process of confession restores our daily *experience* of that forgiveness and ushers in the flow of God's amazing grace and power. We want that.

MIRACULOUS REPAIR KIT: RESTITUTION

We don't only need to ask God to forgive us of our sins, we need to ask those we've sinned against to forgive us. It's called restitution, and I am going to bravely say that I don't believe our healing is complete until it's been accomplished. Jack Frost says it this way, "In order to break that cycle [of reaping what we've sown] and begin restoring trust, it is often necessary to make every effort to bring healing to others and to seek to restore the fractured relationship."[14]

Restitution isn't just saying, "I'm sorry" (often a dutifully quipped selfish statement that's main purpose is often to make *us* feel better); it's more. It's actually asking someone to forgive us, which reveals that we own up to our own guilt. And it puts the control (choice whether to forgive or not) into someone else's hands. This requires a lot of humility on our part. It requires that we become far more concerned with pleasing God than worrying about our own reputation or about how someone is going to react to us. God wants us to make things right with people. Look at what Jesus says in Matthew:

> Therefore if you bring your gift to the altar, and there remember that your brother has something against you, leave your gift there before the altar, and go your way. First be reconciled to your brother, and then come and offer your gift. (Matthew 5:23–24)

God blesses our willingness to take responsibility for our own offenses. Remember what God says He will give us when we are humble? His grace. And His grace is amazingly powerful.

With restitution, we become willing to admit to others where we have failed them. We become willing to confess the wrongs we have committed, no matter how large or small. It may be that my friend is 98 percent wrong in a matter, but I am 100 percent responsible for my 2 percent. Before God, I must do my part.

To go before those I've wronged (my parents, my husband, my children, my pastor, and any others) and ask them—without bringing up one single thing they've done wrong—if they can forgive me for hurting them. And being willing to walk away peacefully no matter the response.

CONTAGIOUS GRACE

Quite often there is a wonderful cycle that is created by restitution. The humility it takes for us to ask for forgiveness has a sort of disarming effect on others, prompting humility in them. Many times I've gone to someone to ask for forgiveness only to be met with the same request from him or her.

Me: "Will you forgive me?"

Him: "Yes, and will you forgive *me*?"

I believe this happens because of the grace God promises to pour out on us when we are humble. That precious grace is powerful enough to spread from us over into the hearts of those around us, and that's when it gets amazing.

If you want to try something really amazing, try getting on your knees before a teenager you've offended and ask for forgiveness. I've done this with my daughter several times. There's nothing quite as amazing as seeing her walls fall down as she sees that I'm willing to admit my faults. It builds trust.

WHEN RESTITUTION ISN'T BEST

Now, there is wisdom to be used in this restitution thing. For example, you would never want to go to someone you've secretly disliked for several years and say, "Pam, I've never liked you. In fact, you've bugged the tar out of me. I know that's wrong of me, and I'd like to ask for your forgiveness." For some reason, I don't see this one going very well. I don't think Pam is going to be at all humbled by the experience. In fact, things will probably get worse.

Before we ever go to anyone with restitution in mind we must pray, pray, pray. We must be sure that it is Holy Spirit-led, with no wrong motivations. It's a great plan to pass the idea by some mature Christian friends just to make sure you're not about to make a huge mistake.

When it's done right, it makes the devil so mad because it restores health to our hearts and relationships in families and churches. And it's the enemy's prime objective to destroy all of that. Let's ruin his plan.

PRAYER OF A VERY THANKFUL HEART

Oh, Precious Jesus,

Thank You does not come close to being the right thing to say for all You have done for me. Your mercy. Your grace. Your forgiveness. They are gifts I know I don't deserve. Your willingness to be broken in every way so that I could be whole is incomprehensible. Words are too feeble to express the praise and honor You deserve.

Holy Spirit, I thank You for taking me on the journey of a lifetime. For tenderly holding my hand and revealing so much truth to me—truth that sets me free. Please never, ever stop. I trust You with my heart completely and give You permission to invade it with Your light. I want to see every blind spot.

And heavenly Father, thank You for forgiving me for all the yucky pride in my heart. For all the judgment and condemnation I cast upon my brothers and sisters in Christ. Please convict me quickly if they ever return. I am so sorry, Lord. I know it grieves Your heart when Your children don't love each other well.

Thank You for my parents. I adore them and ask You to bless them for all the years they put up with my blindness. Thank You for all the people You have put in my life. Each one of them has contributed to who I am today.

Thank You for the gift of forgiveness—receiving it and giving it. Thank You—even though it hurts—for the mental torturers, for their blows pushed me closer to You. Only You would know that it would work that way.

I love You. I surrender to You completely.

Amen

WHAT ABOUT YOU?
FACING FORGIVENESS

1. As you reflect on your daily life, do you feel like you ever deal with "the torturers"? If so, which ones (bitterness, self-pity, entitlement, or others): _____

   _____

   _____

   _____

   _____

2. If you answered "yes" to number one (and you'd be angelic if you didn't), do you think there might be someone you haven't quite forgiven all the way? Maybe a parent, a friend, leader at church, a former boyfriend? Who?

   _____

   _____

   _____

   _____

3. How do you think it would change your life if you became willing to let God take your hand and lead you through the full trek of forgiveness? _____

   _____

   _____

   _____

4. As you reflect further, do you think you've built up sinful defense mechanisms as a result of your pain? For example, because I had a fear of abandonment, I became very possessive and jealous of my friends. I wasn't responsible for the wound, but jealousy is a sin. Do you see anything like this at work in your life? If so, briefly describe: ____

    _____

    _____

    _____

    _____

    _____

    _____

5. After reading chapter 8, do you think there is anyone you might need to ask for forgiveness? Who? _____

    _____

6. If you answered "yes" to number five, what would keep you from asking for forgiveness? _____

    _____

    _____

    _____

    _____

    _____

PEP TALK: WE'RE ALL IN THIS TOGETHER

I don't know about you, but when I have to take difficult steps, it helps me to know I'm not the only one on the journey. This process of forgiving others and asking for our own forgiveness is not a simple pleasure walk down easy street. It's not for the faint of heart, and it's not a solitary venture. We're all on this road trip. We all need mercy.

There is not a single person exempt from needing forgiveness. Every single one of us has failed someone else—most likely many times. And we've all been failed. This is part of the circle of life. (Can you hear *The Lion King* sound track?) With this in mind, don't let the enemy of your soul condemn or shame you for any part of your process. That is his tactic to try to keep you from experiencing the blessing and life that will come as you press through. Keep your eyes focused on our heavenly Father, all the while receiving as much of His love as you can. Before you know it, you'll be standing at the finish line amazed that you were able to run that race.

FORWARD FOCUS: MERCY

- Genesis 39:21—But the LORD was with Joseph and showed him **mercy**, and He gave him favor in the sight of the keeper of the prison.

- Exodus 20:6 — But showing **mercy** to thousands, to those who love Me and keep My commandments.
- Numbers 14:18 — The Lord is longsuffering and abundant in **mercy**, forgiving iniquity and transgression; but He by no means clears the guilty, visiting the iniquity of the fathers on the children to the third and fourth generation.
- Psalm 6:2 — Have **mercy** on me, O LORD, for I am weak; O LORD, heal me, for my bones are troubled.
- Psalm 13:5 — But I have trusted in Your **mercy**; my heart shall rejoice in Your salvation.
- Psalm 86:15 — But You, O Lord, are a God full of compassion, and gracious, longsuffering and abundant in **mercy** and truth.
- Psalm 103:8 — The LORD is **merciful** and gracious, slow to anger, and abounding in mercy.
- Isaiah 49:10 — They shall neither hunger nor thirst, neither heat nor sun shall strike them; for He who has **mercy** on them will lead them, even by the springs of water He will guide them.
- Romans 11:31 — Even so these also have now been disobedient, that through the **mercy** shown you they also may obtain mercy.
- 1 Peter 1:3 — Blessed be the God and Father of our Lord Jesus Christ, who according to His abundant **mercy** has begotten us again to a living hope through the resurrection of Jesus Christ from the dead.
- Jude 1:2 — **Mercy**, peace, and love be multiplied to you.

NINE

UNFINISHED BUSINESS

• • •

I just love the changing of the seasons, don't you? Especially that magical time of year when spring turns the corner into summer and women everywhere prepare themselves for a very important event: finding out if the bathing suit still fits.

And even more fun is opening day at the pool—the day a gal finally gets to strut her stuff (stuff that hasn't seen the light of day in months) for all the neighbors to enjoy. Even though it's wonderful to feel all those eyes on me (not!), I usually like to stay put on my lounge chair reading in the sun. Of course my kids always want me to get in the pool, and I humor them here and there. But I pay the price. Shortly after I get out of the water, my body dries off just enough for my thighs to take on the qualities of double-sided tape, sticking together ever so securely. And swim shorts don't make it any better because they just rise above the stickiness and bunch up at the top of my legs. Lovely.

I'm sure you can tell that bathing suits aren't my favorite attire, but I have to say I owe quite a lot to one special swimsuit. A swimsuit I bought on a special weeklong getaway with Bill.

THE PLAN AND *THE PLAN*

Now before I tell you about the magical bathing suit of wonders, I need to give some background information. Bill and I had set out on this trip to South Carolina in order to attend a weeklong training seminar on helping people deal with wounded hearts and to sneak in some alone time. We were very excited about our plan to learn some helpful information, while at the same time getting some moments on the beach and several date nights.

Trainer had plans for our trip as well.

> **TRAINER:** Do you think there's going to be time for you to get some prayer for yourself at this conference?
>
> **FAT CHRISTIAN WOMAN:** Of course. There will be lots of prayer time.
>
> **TRAINER:** Good, because you definitely need it.
>
> **FAT CHRISTIAN WOMAN:** What do you mean?
>
> **TRAINER:** You are well aware of what I mean. You've got to get help with your fat problem. Someone needs to help you figure out why you can't lose weight.
>
> **FAT CHRISTIAN WOMAN:** Oh, yeah.

TRAINER: It just doesn't make any sense to me that you can be getting all "healed up" (air quotes) in so many ways, yet stay so dang fat. There's got to be a deeply hidden problem with you. Something is very wrong. You definitely need prayer.

FAT CHRISTIAN WOMAN: You're right.

HIDDEN AGENDA

So a trip that started out with a focus on learning how to help others suddenly became all about me. It's kind of like being a perpetual single bridesmaid at a wedding: Even though you're celebrating a friend's blessing, all you can think about is catching that silly bouquet. Surely *this* will be *your* lucky day. Perhaps you might actually meet your Prince Charming.

I couldn't keep my developing agenda hidden for long. For much of our drive to the beach, Bill was informed of my plans for a profound personal breakthrough—the one I had been waiting for all my life. I just knew God was going to reveal the final key to my weight issues, and I would return home a woman with a new metabolism. I could already see myself strutting around in my new skinny jeans, the talk of the town. I was eager for the sessions to begin.

HOLDING MY BREATH

At the end of our first wonderful day of training, the time for personal prayer finally arrived. The men and women all broke off into smaller groups, each with its own leader. I was so excited. I couldn't wait to share my prayer request.

Once my group had found a quiet spot, we all sat in a circle and waited on our leader to start the prayers. A quick assessment of the group told me it would be wise for me to contain myself and allow someone else to go first. I didn't want to appear overly needy and turn everyone off right from the start. After all, I *needed* these people. I was desperate for their insight. A good first impression was essential.

After forcing myself to stay quiet through two other prayer requests (saying "Yes, Lord" at all the appropriate times so as not to appear preoccupied), I finally decided to speak up. I let it all out. In my best "emotionally healthy" voice, I told those women about all the healing I'd been experiencing—healing that had changed my life in every way but one. I still could not lose weight, and because of that I just didn't feel whole.

With as much empathy as they could offer (each woman in my group was thin), they circled around me and began to pray. The prayers were sweet, yet mighty. I held my breath waiting for the moment I'd been anticipating—the moment when my body would be miraculously zapped with a new genetic code (which I would be aware of due to the tingling sensation that would surely accompany this type of transformation).

The last prayer was spoken, and . . . nothing. I felt nothing. But, I told myself it might just take a few days, and lucky for me there were four days left before I had to leave. Surely they'd get their prayers right by then.

STILL NOTHING

The next three days were basically the same as the first, other than the growing feeling of frustration I sensed in my prayer partners. I've sure got to hand it to them; they truly gave it their best prayers, and listening to me drone on and on about my issue couldn't have been their idea of fun.

But nothing was changing. Nothing. Each night at dinner I still found myself desiring dessert (an urge that would surely disappear as a result of my new healing, don't you think?). I still ate every bite of food on my plate, and I still felt fat.

NOT MY IDEA OF FUN

Even though the days weren't turning out to be what I was hoping, Bill and I did get to spend some sweet time together. We walked on the beach and drove around town discussing God's goodness and the new things we were learning. Things weren't all bad. Especially for Bill.

Bill's favorite part of our trip was the inviting pool area our hotel offered. It was surrounded by a lazy river and had an adjacent hot tub (heaven on earth for him) all facing directly out on the ocean. It was pretty cool.

One night after donning his swimsuit and strutting his stuff (stuff that hadn't changed a bit since the day we were married), Bill asked me to come with him down to the hot tub—the last thing in the world I had planned on for the evening. All I really wanted to do was climb into my large sweat pants and under the covers. So, although it was hard to resist the puppy-dog eyes he was giving, I told him I was just too tired. With a pout he kissed my cheek and headed to water wonderland without me.

TRAINER AND THE HUMILIATION SUIT

The next night Bill tried again. Nearly begging this time, Bill asked me to come with him to the hot tub. Knowing that I was his best friend, and feeling guilt at the thought of Bill floating in pathetic isolation, I agreed.

Digging under everything else in my suitcase, I finally found it . . . my humiliation suit (*bathing suit to others*). I hated that stretchy black fabric with its mocking polka dots. Even so, I grabbed it and headed toward the bathroom. (Can you hear the polka dots laughing their heads off already?) I knew who would be waiting for me there. Trainer.

TRAINER: Well, hello. Don't tell me you're actually thinking of going down to the pool.

FAT CHRISTIAN WOMAN: I have to. Bill begged me.

TRAINER: For the life of me, I can't imagine why he'd want to be seen with you. I mean, he's got a perfect body and you . . . well, you don't.

FAT CHRISTIAN WOMAN: Thanks for the vote of confidence.

TRAINER: Well, go ahead. Put on the suit. Let's just get this horror show started.

FAT CHRISTIAN WOMAN: Fine. (*Strips off clothes without looking in mirror.*)

TRAINER: Oh yuck. Quick . . . get your suit on. I can't stand to look at you.

I struggled to get my bathing suit on as quickly as possible, which isn't easy when one must pull and yank while simultaneously gyrating her hips in hopes of instantly decreasing their size. Finally, with the last tug and snap of the shoulder straps and a quick wipe of my brow (this had been a workout), I stood and caught sight of myself in the mirror. Big mistake.

TRAINER: Okay, you're not seriously going to go out in public, are you? I mean, look at yourself. (*Puts hand up to mouth to keep from busting out into a roar of laughter.*)

FAT CHRISTIAN WOMAN: I know. I see it.

TRAINER: Well, your stomach is at least covered, but look at the size of your flabby arms. How did they get that big?

FAT CHRISTIAN WOMAN: I don't know. I'm sorry.

TRAINER: And look at all the dimples in your thighs. Talk about Swiss cheese. Seriously, Teasi, you can't go. You just can't. You're twice the size of Bill.

FAT CHRISTIAN WOMAN: You're right. I am just an

embarrassment to him whether he'll admit it or not.

I'm not going.

I got out of that suit as quickly as I could (doing the reverse gyration move required) and jumped into the safety of my loose-fitting pajama pants. When I finally emerged from the bathroom, the look on Bill's face couldn't hide his disappointment.

"Where's your bathing suit? I thought you were coming with me?"

"I'm sorry. I just can't. I'm too fat. Please just go without me."

Though I know it hurt his feelings, Bill did what I asked. He went to the pool without me yet again. Once the door closed behind him, I went to the bed and cried.

THE DAMASCUS BALCONY

There is a scene in the Bible that is important to me because it's almost exactly what happened to me next.

On his way to persecute more Christians, our brother Saul (later given the name Paul) received a life-changing smack in the face from above. Take a look at the scene:

As he journeyed he came near Damascus, and suddenly a light shone around him from heaven. Then he fell to the ground, and heard a voice saying

to him, "Saul, Saul, why are you persecuting Me?"
And he said, "Who are You, Lord?" Then the Lord
said, "I am Jesus, whom you are persecuting. It
is hard for you to kick against the goads." So he,
trembling and astonished, said, "Lord, what do
You want me to do?" Then the Lord said to him,
"Arise and go into the city, and you will be told
what you must do." (Acts 9:3–6)

After I'd had enough of my own crying, I went out onto
the balcony to give God a piece of my mind.

FAT CHRISTIAN WOMAN: All right, I want answers.
Why did You make me so fat? Why did You give
me such a messed-up metabolism? Why did You
make me so ugly? Why can't I lose weight? (*Persecuting myself.*)

FATHER GOD: (*Silence.*)

FAT CHRISTIAN WOMAN: I drove nearly ten hours
to get some answers—to get to the root of this issue.
Why won't You help me?

FATHER GOD: (*Silence.*)

FAT CHRISTIAN WOMAN: Daddy, please. I need
You to talk to me. I need to know why. Why? Why?

FATHER GOD: (*Silence.*)

FAT CHRISTIAN WOMAN: (*Silence.*)

FATHER GOD: Teasi, Teasi . . . why are you persecuting Me?

FAT CHRISTIAN WOMAN: What do you mean? I'm
not persecuting You.

I sat there stunned for a moment, wondering how God
could say such a thing to me. After all, I had just traveled so
far in order to learn how to help people know Him better.
I loved God with all of my heart—in fact I had no greater
desire than to know Him more.

FAT CHRISTIAN WOMAN: What do you mean? I
love You.

FATHER GOD: You always call me a liar.

FAT CHRISTIAN WOMAN: No, I do not. I totally
believe in Your Word.

FATHER GOD: You don't believe what I say about
you.

FAT CHRISTIAN WOMAN: But that has nothing to
do with my feelings toward You.

FATHER GOD: When you look into the mirror, you
have a choice. You can choose whose opinion you
are going to accept as truth. There are only two
options: My opinion of you, and my enemy, Satan's,
opinion.

FAT CHRISTIAN WOMAN: What about mine? Aren't
I entitled to one of my own?

FATHER GOD: Your opinion will line up with one of the two. There are no other options. All of your life you have believed My enemy. You have been living your life as if what he says about you is truth. This makes My opinion the one you choose not to accept; thus, you have been calling Me a liar.

HYPOCRITICAL OMISSION

Those words acted like that heavenly light that shined down on Saul on that road to Damascus—the one that struck him blind. I wasn't blinded, but I was struck dumb; nothing would come out of my mouth. All I could do was contemplate what had been said to me. Had I been calling God a liar all of my life? Have you?

Isn't it crazy how we pick and choose? It really is nothing less than hypocritical that we find it easy to believe God created the earth, and that Noah was saved on the ark, and that little David killed the giant with a stone, and that Christ rose from the dead. Yet we often refuse to believe that we are fearfully and wonderfully made (Ps. 139:14).

WHAT DADDY SEES

From the very beginning, God has loved His girls. Think about the days of Creation. Everything God made kind of outdid the thing He'd created the day before. He started with night and day, then went on to land and sea, then living things in those places, then fruit trees, and stars, and then man. But

His crowning achievement, His final creation was Eve, our great-grandmother (times several generations, of course). A woman was the finishing touch, and after God made her, He said she was good.

And think of this: God created us to bring forth life. What a purpose! He created us to be nurturers and nourishers of His family. He made us softer than men, more tender and, most often, more emotionally in tune than men. He created us to be a reflection of a large part of His heart, and He adores us. But the devil doesn't.

THE JEALOUS ONE

Satan hates us because he is jealous. You see, he started out his existence beautiful; in fact he was named "son of the morning." Listen to this:

> How you are fallen from heaven, O Lucifer, son of the morning! How you are cut down to the ground, you who weakened the nations! For you have said in your heart: "I will ascend into heaven, I will exalt my throne above the stars of God; I will also sit on the mount of the congregation on the farthest sides of the north; I will ascend above the heights of the clouds, I will be like the most High." (Isaiah 14:12–14)

The devil still wants to outshine us all, and he'll stop at nothing to blind us from our true beauty—from the way God sees His girls.

In her book *Captivating: Unveiling the Mystery of a Woman's Soul*, Stasi Eldredge says, "Satan fell because of his beauty. Now his heart for revenge is to assault beauty. He destroys it in the natural world wherever he can. Strip mines, oil spills, fires, Chernobyl. He wreaks destruction on the glory of God in the earth like a psychopath committed to destroying works of art. But *most* especially, he hates Eve. Because she is captivating, uniquely glorious, and he cannot be. She is the incarnation of the Beauty of God."[15]

Satan doesn't fight fair. He hits us below the belt, wherever it will hurt us the most. He'll stop at nothing to rob us of our true position as God's beauties.

CHOOSING MY TEAM

Thought after thought about what I'd been doing to God all these years took center stage in my mind, and as they did, a righteous sorrow grew in me. How could I have been so cruel to the Lover of my very soul? How could I wear the other team's colors at every game?

I made a decision right then on that balcony that I would do it no more. I knew that I would need the Holy Spirit's power to back up that decision, but I was determined. Things were going to change. I really didn't have a choice. If I was going to call myself a believer, I would have to believe *it all*—

every word that came out of God's mouth. Either that or turn away from it all. I would die before I would do that.

I looked out over the ocean waves shining in the moonlight and turned my heart toward God. Just as Saul had asked on that road to Damascus, I asked the Father, "What would You have me do?" And this is what He said: "Arise, go look into the mirror, and you shall be told what you shall do."

I rose to face my enemy head on.

GOD vs. TRAINER: THE SHOWDOWN

Trainer was there waiting for me, arms crossed over her chest and eyes filled with contempt. I looked right into her eyes, something I had never done before, and stood squarely in front of her. Immediately, she laid into me.

> TRAINER: How dare you look at me like that? Turn those pitiful eyes away from me.

Before I could say a word, someone else answered for me.

> FATHER GOD: I love her blue eyes. They are beautiful to me. I gave them to her so she can behold My wonders.
>
> TRAINER: Too bad they're surrounded by that blotchy face.
>
> FATHER GOD: I love that face. It shines with the reflection of My love when she lets it.

TRAINER: And what about those fat arms? Do you love those?

FATHER GOD: Yes, I gave her those so she could hold My babies and hug My hurting children.

TRAINER: What about that flabby stomach? It's sickening.

FATHER GOD: I love it, for it is there that she carried three of My children, her body being stretched to do so. The marks and extra weight she carries are beautiful to Me.

TRAINER: Well, did you notice the cottage cheese legs she's got?

FATHER GOD: Yes, and I adore those dimples. They are so cute to Me, just as they were when she was a toddler. I gave her those legs so she could carry My love anywhere she wants.

TRAINER: And her wide, wide hips?

FATHER GOD: I love them. Every last inch of her is lovely to Me.

TRAINER: Well, what about—

FATHER GOD: (*Holding up his hand and speaking firmly.*) You are to speak no more. From this moment on, I silence you.

And silence filled the room for several moments after that before God turned with a few more words for me.

> FATHER GOD: From the moment you arise in the morning—every morning—I smile ear to ear, for My sweet girl has awakened to face another day. Please love yourself for Me. You are My glory— My masterpiece—and I love you just as you are.
>
> FAT CHRISTIAN WOMAN: I will, Father. I am so sorry I never have.

As I stood facing that mirror, looking straight into the reflection of my own eyes with fresh vision, I felt the Father's embrace in an almost tangible way. And just before the hug ended, I heard Him whisper one last thing into my soul.

> FATHER GOD: From this moment on you will have a new name. You are never to call yourself a fat Christian woman again. From here on out you are ever and only . . . My Beloved.
>
> BELOVED: (*Looking up into His eyes of pure love.*) And You are mine.

MIRACLE SUIT

Just as He had with Saul, God sent me in a new direction with a new name. Supernaturally, divinely, miraculously . . . the profound personal healing I had set out to get had come. It didn't come the way I thought it would. It was far better.

The day after my encounter on the balcony was the last day of our trip. As we drove back to the hotel from our final training session, I had Bill pull the car over at one of those cute beach shops so I could buy some souvenirs for the kids. But there was something else I purchased: a special tribute to the goodness of God. I bought myself a new bathing suit.

That night Bill went down to the hot tub again . . . only this time, he went with me.

BELOVED'S PRAYER

Father God,

I am so sorry for all the years I called You a liar. I know now that I was hurting You greatly, and I ask You to forgive me for that. You have loved me so tenderly, so completely, and I choose to believe You.

I turn away from believing the lies of the enemy — from believing that what You have created is a mistake. I turn from believing that what You made is malformed or ugly. I turn from believing my value is determined by anything other than what You say.

I am your beloved daughter. An adored princess. Help me, Father, to remember that always. Please come quickly if I ever forget that.

From this moment on I refuse to put the world's opinions above Yours, thinking that beauty is what it deems. You say I am beautiful, and that is my truth.

In Jesus' name,

Amen

WHAT ABOUT YOU?
BEHOLD THE BEAUTY

1. In chapter 1, we started the process of bringing to light our negative self-talk. It is time to deal with those thoughts once and for all. Let's get Trainer in on this. What is something she likes to nag you about? Write it.

    TRAINER: _____

    _____

    _____

    _____

2. Take some time to pray about what Trainer says to you. What does God have to say about all of this? What do you believe He would say to Trainer about this issue?

    GOD (TO TRAINER): _____

    _____

    _____

    _____

    _____

3. What would God say to you about what He sees when He looks at you?

    GOD (TO YOU): _____

    _____

    _____

_____

_____

4. What do you want to say to God about all of this? Do
   you want to see it His way, or do you want to continue to
   believe Trainer?

   YOU: _____

   _____

   _____

5. Part of ending my relationship with Trainer was getting
   rid of my old name (Fat Christian Woman) and accepting
   the new name God had for me, "Beloved." What do you
   think your old name was? What is your new name?

   a. **Old name:**_____

   b. **New name:** _____

PEP TALK: CHOOSE GOD'S DEFINITION

There are as many different definitions of beauty as there are
locations on the map. In some countries, the fatter a woman
is, the more beautiful she is declared. There are places where
altered skull shape is beautiful and the more body piercings
the better. There are so many *human* definitions of what is

beautiful that one could go crazy trying to figure out which one is best. That's why we need to look at the one true definition: God's definition.

The Bible is so clear about God's attraction to the things of the heart. Yes, He is the creator of external beauty, but nothing is more beautiful to Him than a heart that is fully submitted to Him. Think about this: Jesus Himself wasn't considered a handsome man. The Bible says that if we saw Him, we wouldn't desire Him based on looks (Isa. 53:2). Also, the apostle Paul is said to be very awkward looking—short and bald with bushy eyebrows. If nothing else, this should tell us to get out there and get going. We must never let the world's definition of beauty (and our perceived lack in this area) keep us from being mighty warriors for our God.

FORWARD FOCUS: BEAUTY

- 1 Chronicles 16:29—Give to the LORD the glory due His name; bring an offering, and come before Him. Oh, worship the LORD in the **beauty** of holiness!
- Psalm 27:4—One thing I have desired of the LORD, that will I seek: that I may dwell in the house of the LORD all the days of my life, to behold the **beauty** of the LORD, and to inquire in His temple.
- Psalm 45:11—So the King will greatly desire your **beauty**; because He is your Lord, worship Him.

- Psalm 90:17 — And let the **beauty** of the LORD our God be upon us, and establish the work of our hands for us; yes, establish the work of our hands.
- Psalm 96:6 — Honor and majesty are before Him; strength and **beauty** are in His sanctuary.
- Psalm 33:1 — Rejoice in the LORD, O you righteous! For praise from the upright is **beautiful**.
- Proverbs 31:30 — Charm is deceitful and **beauty** is passing, but a woman who fears the LORD, she shall be praised.
- Romans 10:15 — And how shall they preach unless they are sent? As it is written: "How **beautiful** are the feet of those who preach the gospel of peace, who bring glad tidings of good things!"
- James 1:11 — For no sooner has the sun risen with a burning heat than it withers the grass; its flower falls, and its **beautiful** appearance perishes. So the rich man also will fade away in his pursuits.
- 1 Peter 3:4 — Rather let it be the hidden person of the heart, with the incorruptible **beauty** of a gentle and quiet spirit, which is very precious in the sight of God.

TEN

DEFENDING TERRITORY

I may never march down your runways,
Wear your bikinis,
Be on your magazines;
I may never fit your ideal for me,
But I'm in the Lord's Army,
Yes, sir!
(To the tune of "I'm in the Lord's Army")

•••

Many a battle has been won or lost in the pursuit of acquiring land—in fighting for a physical territory. Once the war has been won, however, the winning side better not lay down their weapons or they might lose what they fought so hard to gain. Well, the same is really true in our own lives. Any emotional or spiritual territory we win for the Lord must be defended daily. The losing team isn't going to give up quickly. In fact, its leader is a very sore loser.

We can't say God didn't warn us. He is pretty honest in His Word when He tells us that we're going to have trouble in this life. John 16:33 says, "These things I have spoken to you, that in Me you may have peace. In the world you will have tribulation; but be of good cheer, I have overcome the world." The good news is the last part: God is the ultimate winner, and because we are His kids, we win too.

EASY TO FORGET

But even though we know how the big story ends, it's easy for us to get lost in the struggles and distractions of our life now. It's easy to forget God's epic plan as we sort through never-ending piles of laundry. It's easy to forget we are children of the King when we compare our own anticlimactic Facebook status to those of our "friends"—friends who all seem to be living the high life. And it's easy to be tricked into loosening our hold on what God has given us when we take "just a peek" at the new real-estate listings—including the dream house we will never be able to afford.

Why is it so easy to forget? Because we're human. We come by our forgetfulness honestly. After all, we inherited it from our first parents, Adam and Eve. How quickly they forgot how good they had it.

FIREPOWER

We aren't helpless victims of our human limitations, praise God. We have a powerful weapon—one that is more than capable of giving us the firepower we need to protect our land. The weapon is God's truth. No matter how tempting it may be to believe the lying voices that try to take center stage in our heads, we've got to be intentional about shutting them up. Their only mission is to make our lives miserable on the journey—while we live out our lives here on earth in anticipation of the ultimate victory to come in eternity.

When you really get to the bottom of it all, God's truth is the ultimate healer of our every wound. It is the key that opens our prison door. It is the light that expels every bit of darkness in our hearts, revealing the things that have kept us repeating self-defeating cycles.

Defending territory ultimately comes down to this question: do you believe God's truth? That comes more naturally as we begin to see the proof working out in our lives, but it also gets easier when we are better at identifying lies. And that becomes simpler as we expose the author of all lies, Satan.

CHIEF LIAR: SATAN

The Bible has many ways of describing God's ultimate enemy. The father of lies (John 8:44), the accuser of the brethren (Rev. 12:10), adversary (1 Pet. 5:8), beast (Rev. 14:9–10), deceiver (Rev. 12:9), devil (1 John 3:8), evil one (John 17:15), ruler of darkness (Eph. 6:12), and so many more. The only descriptor we need for him, however, is this: disarmed (Col. 2:15). He is a defeated foe. A loser. The truth is he's a weakling. The only power he has is pretend power, and the only time it works for him is when we believe his lies.

So he works really hard at making his lies convincing. He's even got them tailor-made for each one of us. He knows your weaknesses. If you're struggling to trust God with your finances, he'll tell you things like this: "You're never going to have anything. You're always going to be flat broke." If you're working through trusting your friends, he'll tell you things like this: "She doesn't really like you. It's not safe to open up to her." He works overtime when he can see that we're physically worn down, and, if you are female, he especially loves "that time of the month."

NOT A KNOW-IT-ALL

But, the devil really isn't "all that." For many years I thought that Satan was quite powerful. I thought he could read my mind just like God can, but that's not true. Satan is not omnipotent (all-knowing), nor is he omnipresent (everywhere at once). He is a created being just as we are. He's got limitations, but he doesn't want us to know about them.

His limitations require him to enlist an army of helpers. These happen to be the fallen angels the Bible tells us about (2 Pet. 2:4; Jude 1:6). The Bible describes this whole team in Ephesians 6:12:

> For we do not wrestle against flesh and blood, but against principalities, against powers, against the rulers of the darkness of this age, against spiritual hosts of wickedness in the heavenly places.

It's clear that there is a team at work against us, and each member is a great student of human behavior. Sometimes I wonder if there are certain demons assigned to just me. All my life they've been watching me so they can really know my weaknesses. How else would they know exactly when to strike?

SATAN'S BIGGEST PUPPET: SOCIETY

Even though it's hard to believe, the Bible calls Satan the god of this age (2 Cor. 4:4). In many ways he's been given permission to do as he pleases—but not for long. Now, he doesn't have power to control us when we have Christ in us, but it is very easy for him to capitalize on the blindness of the lost and the blind spots of believers. All he needs to do is whisper a lie here and there, and soon millions of unsuspecting victims become his closest allies.

These blind victims compose our society, and the devil uses it to hurt us wherever he can. Billboards scream against the things that please God. Nearly every quarter of a mile a large-breasted, scantily clad woman on a huge poster tries to convince God's sons to take a quick turn off the straight and narrow road into "paradise." Talk show hosts spout their "expert" opinion on what God is really like saying, "Surely any *good* god would accept everyone into heaven." Yes, Satan is the king of propaganda.

LOW BLOW: OUR LOOKS

His all-time favorite way to use society against us is to have it define beauty—a pile of lies that destroys the multitudes. It hurts so many because so few actually fit into the world's slim definition of what we should look like. And it hurts us because for the most part, our looks aren't something we have much control over (excluding surgery and loads of makeup).

Most importantly of all, the devil likes to try to make us focus most on what matters to God the least—our outward appearance. God really wants us focusing on the condition of our hearts so that we can tap into the real joy and the real life He has for us. Listen to what the Bible says:

- Give to the LORD the glory due His name; bring an offering, and come before Him. Oh, worship the LORD in the beauty of holiness! (1 Chronicles 16:29)
- Charm is deceitful and beauty is passing, but a woman who fears the LORD, she shall be praised. (Proverbs 31:30)
- Do not let your adornment be merely outward—arranging the hair, wearing gold, or putting on fine apparel—rather let it be the hidden person of the heart, with the incorruptible beauty of a gentle and quiet spirit, which is very precious in the sight of God. (1 Peter 3:3–4)

God's definition of beauty has far more to do with what's going on inside of us than what's skin deep. In fact, a search of the Bible will reveal no mention of body mass index, no mention of normal weight charts, no mention of point values for foods. Not only that, almost any time the word *fat* is mentioned, it's used as a *good thing*—representing blessing.

Now, of course God wants us healthy. Just because our bodies are not the *most* important thing to Him doesn't mean they aren't important *at all*. There is no scriptural justification for allowing our bodies to grow morbidly obese. The Bible is clear that we are to have no other gods before the true God, and that includes food (Ex. 20:3). If we are dangerously overweight (and it's not due to a medical condition over which we have little control), there is a good chance we are turning to the Oreos for comfort a bit too often, and that's a role God wants to fill.

CARRYING THE GOODS

The true purpose of our body—God's purpose—is to be a dwelling place for His Spirit on earth and to carry His love to a hurting world.

> Or do you not know that your body is the temple
> of the Holy Spirit who is in you, whom you have
> from God, and you are not your own? For you
> were bought at a price; therefore glorify God in

your body and in your spirit, which are God's. (1
Corinthians 6:19–20)

To "glorify" God with our body means to use it to honor
or magnify Him. There are many ways to interpret what that
might look like in our individual lives. But one thing is for
sure, we can't do it if we hate our body so much that we keep
it hidden from the world in shame. That's the devil's goal.
How do you think he's doing?

Our enemy wants us to be so ashamed of the appearance of our body that we forget all about the life-changing
potential (God's Spirit) it houses. If he can influence us to
become embarrassed enough, maybe we'll just stay home
and keep that good stuff to ourselves. (*I'm not going because
my pants are too tight.*) And when we do, it just leaves more
hurting people—maybe even a family member or friend—to
die without hope.

SUIT UP

In addition to getting good at identifying lies, we've got
to armor up every day if we're going to win our battle of
defending territory. God has our protective clothing laid out
for us ready for the taking.

Therefore take up the whole armor of God, that
you may be able to withstand in the evil day, and
having done all, to stand. Stand therefore, having

girded your waist with truth, having put on the breastplate of righteousness, and having shod your feet with the preparation of the gospel of peace; above all, taking the shield of faith with which you will be able to quench all the fiery darts of the wicked one. And take the helmet of salvation, and the sword of the Spirit, which is the word of God; praying always with all prayer and supplication in the Spirit, being watchful to this end with all perseverance and supplication for all the saints. (Ephesians 6:13–18)

First we have our spiritual Spanx, the belt of truth. This holds everything securely together and creates a smooth (no panty lines) foundation for all the other pieces of our kingdom attire.

Next we have our Wonderbra, the breastplate of righteousness. Just as this handy undergarment disguises what we may be lacking in the bosom area (thank you, push-up technology), our spiritual breastplate hides what we are lacking in righteousness. It reminds us that from the time we accept Christ as our Savior, His righteousness becomes our own (1 Cor. 1:30). The enemy will always try to tell us, "You're not righteous." When he does, we can simply say, "You're right. But Jesus is. And my life is now hidden in Him. So there!"

Once our upper body is taken care of, we can slip our beautiful feet into a confidence-boosting pair of heels, our shoes of peace (move over, Prada). In these, we can boldly take the good news anywhere God leads, fearing nothing. "For God has not given us a spirit of fear, but of power and of love and of a sound mind" (2 Tim. 1:7).

Then we want to grab a purse, our shield of faith. Now we don't want a cute little clutch here. No, we want the biggest, sturdiest purse we can find—one that when held out in front of us would take a bullet. Just as with a purse, our shield of faith grows larger the more "stuff" we put in. As we study God's Word more and experience more of Him in our daily lives, our shield becomes more substantial. The bigger the better.

And of course, no woman I know is going to leave the house without checking her hair. (I can't believe how bad my roots are.) Now, as Christians, we've got something far more dazzling to cover our heads than those lovely locks; we've got our helmet of salvation (Eph. 6:17). This divine accessory declares to the enemy that we belong eternally to God because we have been bought with a high price.

And finally we've got to put some lipstick on those luscious lips because they've got some work to do; they've got to proclaim the Word of God. This is our only offensive weapon as Christians, our sword of the Spirit. In the Greek definition, this usage of *word* means specifically the spoken

Word of God. Remember, our enemy can't read our minds, so we need to tell him verbally to back off. (Don't worry about what the family will think—you know Mom hasn't lost her mind.) Just proclaim the truth out loud. Even if you're the only one around. Joyce Meyer says this, "In order to overcome the negative thinking and speaking that have been such a natural part of our lifestyle for so long, we must make a conscious effort to think and speak good things about ourselves to ourselves by making positive confessions."[16] And listen to this: "With the heart one believes unto righteousness, and with the mouth confession is made unto salvation" (Rom. 10:10). Get talking, girl.

FIGHTING IN THE MEAN . . . TIME

Now, in the physical world, it might be important to spend lots of time studying one's enemy. Learning everything about it—the enemy's inner workings, and ultimate plans. But, in the kingdom of God, it really doesn't work that way. In God's world, we win our battle against the enemy by focusing not on the devil, but on God. The more we set our hearts and minds on the things above, the more powerful we are against our foe (Col. 3:2; James 4:7).

And setting our sights on things above means remembering that this world is not our home (Heb. 11:13). We are strangers in this world, and our ultimate destiny will not be fulfilled until we are sitting in our heavenly Father's literal presence looking at Him face to face. What an amazing day that will be!

In the meantime, as we wait for that nice time, we must establish a strategy for daily success. The devil will try to keep us overburdened by the cares and pain of the temporary. But we must not be tricked. The more you can be proactive instead of reactive, the better.

- Tape your favorite scriptures to your bathroom mirror and commit them to heart.
- Play worship music often.
- Read your Bible and as many uplifting and encouraging books as you can get your hands on.
- Have at least one good friend you can be totally real with—one who won't doubt your salvation when you let it all out. (External processing to the rescue.)
- Go to bed early sometimes (I've called it a day as early as 4:30 p.m. on occasion), and remember that His mercies are new every morning.
- Never hesitate to get professional help when all the above doesn't seem to be cutting it.

SILENCE THE COMMUNITY

You may not have Trainer (the voice that berated my body) or Reflection (the one who calls out my moral weakness) or Sabby (who wants to sabotage everything) living in your head. The fruits and veggies might not throw snide remarks your way at the grocery store. But, I'll bet you have some not-so-kind voices trying to be heard in that head of yours. Any voices that don't encourage you in the truth must be silenced.

I know from experience that some of these voices don't give up easily. Even after experiencing great healing in my life, Reflection tries to tear me down here and there. I just tell her to shut it. Sabby likes to try to get me off the beaten path with her self-absorbed ideas and selfish motivations. I have to tell her to shut up too. The more times I tell them to zip it, the less they try to speak. They've just kind of given up.

Miraculously, I never hear from Trainer any more. God pretty much zipped her lip once and for all. I have never equated my value with the appearance of my body (no matter what my weight) since that encounter at the beach. Sometimes God just does the really big stuff for us. It's the miracle of a transformed heart.

EMBRACE LIFE

There is one very important truth you must always remember: your life matters. Yours, mine, everyone's . . . God planned them all before the beginning of time (Ps. 139:16). He formed us in our mother's wombs with a purpose in mind (Ps. 139:13). Not one of us is a mistake.

No matter the circumstances of our birth—whether we were conceived in the back of a car during a teenage lust fest, or in the marriage bed of a happily married couple—God is the one who delivered us and brought us into the world. We truly are His children. We were His idea.

The one thing our enemy wants most of all is to see us dead (John 10:10). So, we must not let him succeed. Let's choose to embrace life—the good and the bad of it, remembering that even when life is painful, God is at work. He is the Master Gardener in our lives, and as Bunny Wilson says in the book, *Becoming God's True Woman*, "The gardener only prunes the branches that belong to him, which makes it an honor."[17] Let's give the Father praise for all He's done to redeem the messes we've been a part of, whether willingly or not.

> For we are His workmanship, created in Christ Jesus for good works, which God prepared beforehand that we should walk in them. (Ephesians 2:10)

A VICTORY PRAYER

Precious Father,

Thank You for being a God of love and for pouring that love upon me. Thank You that Your Word is steady and unchanging and that it is a rock for me to stand on in every season of my life.

Thank You for healing my brokenness. Continue to show me the places in my heart that still need Your touch. Thank You for giving me everything I need to rise above the hurts in my life and the plan of my enemy to hurt me. You are such a good God.

I thank You for the territory You have given me—my inheri-

tance in Christ. I pray for the wisdom to defend it. Help me to recognize the lies I hear in my head and to use my weapon of Your truth against them . . . quickly. I give You permission to convict me every time I forget all You have done in my life, giving opportunity for Satan to steal Your glory.

Thank You for my life—every bit of it. I know You planned it, and You long to direct it. Thank You that You have promised to complete the good work You've started in me as I surrender to Your plans. I want to be a warrior for You, Father—a warrior for truth.

I pray that Your voice would drown out all the others in my head, that I would become more and more sensitive to Your Spirit so that I can love others better. Show me what matters most to You in my every day so that I can be a part of it.

All that I am is for You. There is nothing I want more than to be loved by You and give Your love away. I am ruined for the ordinary.

In the name of Jesus, my amazing Lord.

Amen

HOW ABOUT YOU?
BEATING THE BEAST

1. How can you tell if a thought is a lie? _____

_____

_____

2. If you catch yourself believing a lie in the future, what will you do? What is your plan of attack? _____

_____

_____

3. Why do we want to proclaim the truth aloud? _____

_____

_____

4. List a couple of truths you want to commit to memory
   so that you have your ammunition ready at all times (for
   example, *No weapon formed against me shall prosper*):

   a. _____

   _____

   _____

   b. _____

   _____

   _____

5. Have you been keeping your "delivery truck" parked in
   the garage too often? If so, do you think you can take
   steps toward taking it for a spin more often? _____

   _____

   _____

   _____

PEP TALK: IN IT TO WIN IT

This Christian journey is not for wimps. This is a life for warriors—for those who intend to go for the gusto. The good news is we've been given all the supplies we need to run this race to the finish. We will never find ourselves lacking.

I don't know about you, but I don't want to settle for anything less than God's best for me. I've done that before, and it's anticlimactic. I don't want to settle down just because I've secured my salvation from hell. No. I want to live an adventure for God—battling the enemy to the death for my King. I don't want to listen to Satan's junk. I don't want to give him the time of day. And not only that . . . I want to get back from him everything he's stolen from me in the past. I want my full inheritance. I know you want yours too. We've got to take the advice given by the unorthodox newsman in the movie *Network*: We've got to stand up to the devil and say, "I'm as mad as hell, and I'm not going to take this anymore."

FORWARD FOCUS: VICTORY

- 2 Samuel 23:10—He arose and attacked the Philistines until his hand was weary, and his hand stuck to the sword. The LORD brought about a great **victory** that day; and the people returned after him only to plunder.

- 1 Chronicles 29:11—Yours, O LORD, is the greatness, the power and the glory, the **victory** and the majesty; for all that is in heaven and in earth is Yours; Yours is the kingdom, O LORD, and You are exalted as head over all.
- Psalm 98:1—Oh, sing to the LORD a new song! For He has done marvelous things; His right hand and His holy arm have gained Him the **victory**.
- Matthew 12:20—A bruised reed He will not break, and smoking flax He will not quench, till He sends forth justice to **victory**.
- 1 Corinthians 15:54—So when this corruptible has put on incorruption, and this mortal has put on immortality, then shall be brought to pass the saying that is written: "Death is swallowed up in **victory**."
- 1 Corinthians 15:55—O Death, where is your sting? O Hades, where is your **victory**?
- 1 Corinthians 15:57—But thanks be to God, who gives us the **victory** through our Lord Jesus Christ.
- 1 John 5:4—For whatever is born of God overcomes the world. And this is the **victory** that has overcome the world—our faith.
- Revelation 15:2—And I saw something like a sea of glass mingled with fire, and those who have the **victory** over the beast, over his image and over his mark and over the number of his name, standing on the sea of glass, having harps of God.

CONCLUSION

God has such a great sense of humor, don't you think? His ways are often so contrary to our own, and I love that.

As I look back at my life, I see that the thing I wanted for so many years — the thing I thought would make my life worth living might have actually killed me. If I had been the skinny woman I was desperate to be, I would have had a beautiful body, but that's about all. I know myself, and I know that if I had always been satisfied with my looks, I would have found my full value in that. I would have happily strutted my stuff, enjoying the attention it brought me. But I wouldn't have known the goodness of God like I do today.

God wants us for Himself. He wants us to want Him above all else, and He wants to perform miracles in our lives. I love how Nancy DeMoss puts it. She says, "God specializes in the impossible, so that when the victory is won and the task is complete, we cannot take any credit."[18]

I can almost hear the conversation that must have gone on in heaven when God was designing me. "This daughter of mine is going to love beauty, but I want her to love MY beauty, so I'm going to put a little extra padding on her to keep her from being vain. Vanity would kill her."

I'm not sure if that's exactly how it happened, but I do know this: my padded body is one of the biggest blessings in my life. If I had not been so utterly desperate to get answers about my big rear, I don't know that I would have ever found out what I really needed. I don't know that I would have seen how very little of God's love I was really experiencing or how selfish my love for others had been. Chances are, I would have been a wounded skinny chick, pretty on the outside but broken on the inside.

Ironically, whatever it is that you despise most about yourself (it doesn't have to be weight) can become the catalyst for serious life change. Take that "thing" and drop it down at the feet of Jesus. Then ask Him to help you get to the bottom of it. But be willing to *really* get to the bottom of it. The answer you get might not be the one you've wanted or expected, but it will be the one you *need*.

I'm still "padded" today, but I love myself more than I ever have because I no longer let the devil define me. I let my doctors (not *Vanity Fair* or *Cosmo*) tell me if I'm physically healthy, and I let God alone assign my value. And truthfully, as long as I'm healthy, if I never lost a pound I'd be more than fine with that. In fact, if someone were to offer me a pill right now—one that would assure me a thin body for the rest of my life no matter what I ate, with only one stipulation: you must give up all the hope and healing you've gained on the inside—I would laugh and walk away. Being thinner is nothing compared to being free.

I believe it can happen for you too. Your pain can be turned into dancing as you stand under the waterfall of the Father's amazing love. And when it does, your testimony will be used as a powerful part of God's plan to overcome Satan. Look at this:

> And they overcame him [the evil one] by the blood
> of the Lamb and by the word of their testimony.
> (Revelation 12:11)

Let's stand together as daughters of the King and tell our stories to all who will listen. Once we carried a load of pain and shame and despair, but God knew exactly how to use that burden. He knew exactly how to bring beauty out of those ashes. He knew that in the end it would all be worth the weight.

FINAL PRAYER

Father God,
> *Thank YOU for my big bottom.*
> *I love You. And I can't wait until I can tell You that face to face.*
> *Amen*

RECOMMENDED RESOURCES

There are many quality books and ministries that provide resources that deal with the issues I have touched on in this book. I highly recommend that you not stop here. If any of the topics resonated with you, continue to search it out. I can, however, highly recommend the following list of resources for further insight and encouragement in your journey toward God's best life for you.

To the best of my knowledge, I believe these resources are faithful to Scripture, and they have all been a blessing to me personally. However, inclusion in this list does not necessarily imply my complete endorsement of the authors, resources, or organizations represented. As Christians, it is our duty to personally examine everything in the light of God's Word.

Anderson, Neil. *The Bondage Breaker*. Eugene, OR: Harvest House, 2000.

Backus, William, and Marie Chapian. *Telling Yourself the Truth*. Bloomington, MN: Bethany House, 2000.

Cloud, Henry, and John Townsend. *Boundaries: When to Say Yes, How to Say No, to Take Control of Your Life*. Grand Rapids: Zondervan, 1992.

DeMoss, Nancy. *Becoming God's True Woman*. Wheaton, IL: Crossway Books, 2008.

Eldredge, John, and Stasi Eldredge. *Captivating*. Nashville: Thomas Nelson, 2005.

Frost, Jack. *Experiencing the Father's Embrace*. Shippensburg, PA: Destiny Image, 2004.

Frost, Jack. *Spiritual Slavery to Spiritual Sonship: Your Destiny Awaits You*. Shippensburg, PA: Destiny Image, 2006.

Hession, Roy. *The Calvary Road*. London: Christian Literature Crusade, 1950.

Meyer, Joyce. *Straight Talk: Overcoming Emotional Battles with the Power of God's Word*. New York, New York: Time Warner Book Group, 2004.

Mullen, Grant. *Emotionally Free: a Prescription for Healing Body, Soul and Spirit*. Tonbridge, England: Sovereign World, 2003.

Murray, Andrew. *Humility: the Journey Toward Holiness*. Bloomington, MN: Bethany House, 2001.

Rhodes, Constance. *Life Inside the "Thin" Cage: A Personal Look into the Hidden World of the Chronic Dieter*. Colorado Springs, CO: WaterBrook Press, 2003.

Wilson, Sandra. *Hurt People Hurt People*. Grand Rapids: Discovery House Books, 2001.

Winter, Jack. *The Homecoming: Unconditional Love: Finding Your Place in the Father's Heart*. Seattle: YWAM Publishing, 1997.

APPENDIX A

ORPHAN VS. CHILD OF GOD

ORPHAN HEART		HEART OF GOD'S CHILD
See God as Master	IMAGE OF GOD	See God as a loving Father
Independent/self-reliant	DEPENDENCY	Interdependent/ acknowledges need
Live by the love of law	THEOLOGY	Live by the law of love
Insecure/lack peace	SECURITY	Rest and peace
Strive for the praise, approval, and acceptance of people	NEED FOR APPROVAL	Totally accepted in God's love and justified by grace
A need for personal achievement as I seek to impress God and others, or no motivation to serve at all	MOTIVE FOR SERVICE	Service that is motivated by a deep gratitude for being unconditionally loved and accepted by God
Duty and earning God's favor, or no motivation at all	MOTIVE BEHIND CHRISTIAN DISCIPLINES	Pleasure and delight

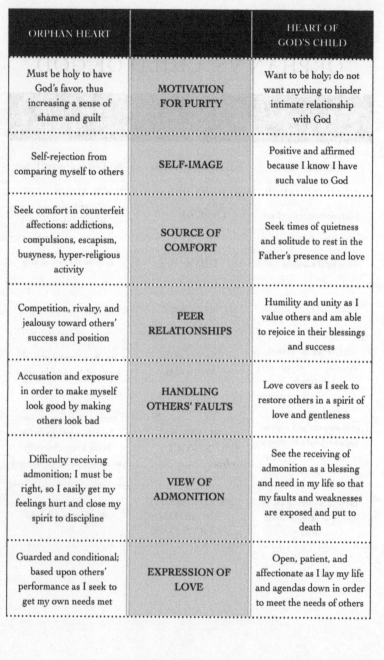

ORPHAN HEART		HEART OF GOD'S CHILD
Must be holy to have God's favor, thus increasing a sense of shame and guilt	**MOTIVATION FOR PURITY**	Want to be holy; do not want anything to hinder intimate relationship with God
Self-rejection from comparing myself to others	**SELF-IMAGE**	Positive and affirmed because I know I have such value to God
Seek comfort in counterfeit affections: addictions, compulsions, escapism, busyness, hyper-religious activity	**SOURCE OF COMFORT**	Seek times of quietness and solitude to rest in the Father's presence and love
Competition, rivalry, and jealousy toward others' success and position	**PEER RELATIONSHIPS**	Humility and unity as I value others and am able to rejoice in their blessings and success
Accusation and exposure in order to make myself look good by making others look bad	**HANDLING OTHERS' FAULTS**	Love covers as I seek to restore others in a spirit of love and gentleness
Difficulty receiving admonition; I must be right, so I easily get my feelings hurt and close my spirit to discipline	**VIEW OF ADMONITION**	See the receiving of admonition as a blessing and need in my life so that my faults and weaknesses are exposed and put to death
Guarded and conditional; based upon others' performance as I seek to get my own needs met	**EXPRESSION OF LOVE**	Open, patient, and affectionate as I lay my life and agendas down in order to meet the needs of others

ORPHAN HEART		HEART OF GOD'S CHILD
Conditional and distant	**SENSE OF GOD'S PRESENCE**	Close and intimate
Bondage	**CONDITION**	Liberty
Feel like a servant/slave	**POSITION**	Feel like a son/daughter
Spiritual ambition; the earnest desire for some spiritual achievement and distinction and the willingness to strive for it; a desire to be seen and counted among the mature	**VISION**	To daily experience the Father's unconditional love and acceptance and then be sent as a representative of His love to family and others
Fight for what I can get!	**FUTURE**	Relationship as a child releases my inheritance!
See authority as a source of pain; distrustful toward them and lacking a heart attitude of submission	**VIEW OF AUTHORITY**	Respectful, honoring; I see them as ministers of God for good in my life

(Chart adapted by permission from Shiloh Place Ministry training materials.)[19]

APPENDIX B

PERSONALITY TYPES THAT CAN DEVELOP WHEN WE'RE EMOTIONALLY WOUNDED

1) The "Show-off"

To get our emotional needs met, we draw as much attention to ourselves as possible. We become very talkative, trying to make ourselves look important by name-dropping, exaggerating our accomplishments in work, sports, ministry, or family. We can't help but steer nearly all conversations back to ourselves.

2) The "People Pleaser"

We find our identity in conforming to group ideals. We have very little, if any, identity of our own, so we conform to the perceived norm in order to belong. We fit into groups well because we are good at saying the right things to be accepted. At church we are the perfect Christian, but with our non-Christian friends, we fit right in too. We can be fairly critical of others, but cannot receive criticism from others.

3) The "Timid"

We are not to be confused with the meek (which is a character strength). We have a big fear of man, failure, and rejection.

We lack the inner strength to make our own decisions. We usually deal with self-pity and a sense of no self-worth. Most people don't know, but deep inside of us there is often quite a bit of anger. We are usually very passive.

4) The "Isolationist"
Our inner pain has caused us to form walls of self-protection. We cut ourselves off from anyone we think is a threat to us and we usually bond to only one or two people. This can cause us to become very possessive of those we get close to and to feel threatened by anyone else entering into our relationships.

5) The "Fighter"
We become rebellious and defiant towards everyone and everything, especially the system we presently have to operate in. We are usually very independent because we don't want to have to depend on anyone who may hurt us again. Often, we become workaholics in order to prove our self-worth and to establish our identity.

6) The "Moralist"
We are God's policemen. We see the fault in everything and everyone and know how to fix it. We have an answer for everything under the sun. We are very opinionated, which

reveals our lack of humility. We live by the letter of the law but are empty of love. We are usually right in our observations, but have the wrong attitude; that makes us wrong. However, to us, our rightness justifies our wrong attitude.

(Adapted by permission from Shiloh Place Ministries training materials.)

NOTES

1. Shaun Dreisbach "Shocking Body Image News," *Glamour*, March 2011, http://www.glamour.com/health-fitness/2011/02/shocking-body-image-news -97-percent-of-women-will-be-cruel-to-their-bodies-today

2. "Body Image Statistics," Find Your True Beauty, http://www.findyour truebeauty.com

3. U.S. Census Bureau News, "Unmarried and Single Americans Week Sept 19-25, 2010" news release, July 19, 2010, http://www.census.gov/news-room/releases/pdf/cb10ff-18_single.pdf

4. "Cosmetic Surgery," About-face, http://about-face.org/r/facts/cosmetic surgery.shtml#consumers

5. Ranlyn Oakes, "Diet Industry Facts," LiveStrong.com, August 17, 2010, http://www.livestrong.com/article/207926-diet-industry-facts/

6. Sandra Wilson, *Hurt People Hurt People* (Grand Rapids: Discovery House, 2001), 21.

7. "Child Abuse in America," http://www.childhelp.org/pages/statistics

8. Jack Frost, *Spiritual Slavery to Spiritual Sonship*, (Shippensburg, PA: Destiny Image, 2006), 37.

9. "The Leadership Survey on Pastors and Internet Pornography," *Leadership Journal*, Winter 2001, http://www.christianitytoday.com/le/2001/ winter/12.89.html

10. Wilson, *Hurt People*, 35.

11. William Backus and Marie Chapman, *Telling Yourself the Truth* (Grand Rapids: Bethany House, 2000), 15.

12. Tim Clinton and Ron Hawkins, *The Quick-Reference Guide to Biblical Counseling* (Grand Rapids: Baker Books, 2009), 123.

13. Alex Harris and Carl Thoresen, "Forgiveness, Unforgiveness, Health and Disease," ed. E. L. Worthington Jr. (New York:Brunner-Routledge, 2005), 324, in *Handbook of Forgiveness*, http://www.chce.research.va.gov/docs/pdfs/ pi_publications/Harris/2005_Harris_Thorsen_HF.pdf

14. Frost, *Spiritual Slavery*, 215 .

15. John Eldredge and Stasi Eldredge, *Captivating: Unveiling the Mystery of a Woman's Soul* (Nashville: Thomas Nelson, 2005), 84.

16. Joyce Meyer, *Straight Talk: Overcoming Emotional Battles with the Power of God's Word* (New York: Warner Faith, 2004), 263.

17. P. Bunny Wilson, "Pruned to Bloom" in *Becoming God's True Woman*, ed. Nancy Leigh DeMoss (Wheaton, IL: Crossway Books, 2008), 99.

18. Nancy Leigh DeMoss, "Portrait of a Woman Used by God" in *Becoming God's True Woman*, 68.

19. Training materials used by permission from Shiloh Place Ministries, Conway, SC (http://www.shilohplace.org).

Teasi Cannon is married to her best friend, Bill, and they have three awesome children: Carli, Ben, and Sam. Teasi has a masters degree in pastoral counseling from Liberty Theological Seminary and is a sought-after speaker and conference leader based in Nashville, Tennessee, who loves to help women remember who they are in Christ.